2024 LEVEL UP

100% UNOFFICIAL

BY GAMERS FOR GAMERS

SCHOLASTIC

GET READY TO LEVEL UP!

Has there ever been a better time to be a gamer? This year, we've seen amazing new games in the *Legend of Zelda*, *Street Fighter*, and *Pokémon* series, plus some awesome *Star Wars* and *Marvel* titles. There have been spectacular comebacks from *Sonic the Hedgehog* and *Need for Speed*, and new ways to explore the worlds of Disney and Harry Potter. We can hunt monsters, battle dinosaurs, farm strange critters, or explore alien worlds. And there's even more exciting stuff around the corner.

From big console hits to tiny indie games, virtual reality to mobile gaming, the world of gaming continues to expand, and a game you hadn't heard of yesterday could become your next obsession! Take this book as your guide to this world—and the skills and tactics that will help you beat your favorite games!

STAY SAFE AND HAVE FUN!

■ Games are brilliant, but you need to know how to stay safe while you're playing, especially when you're online. Follow these simple rules to have a great time!

1 Talk to your parents and work out some rules about which games you can play, when you can play them, and if you can play them online.

2 Never give out any personal information while you're gaming, including your real name, where you live, your parents' names, where you go to school, any passwords, or your phone number. Don't ever agree to meet someone you've met online or through a game in person.

3 Tell your parents or a teacher if you come across something online that makes you feel uncomfortable.

4 Be nice to other players, even when you're competing against them. Don't say anything that might hurt someone's feelings or make them feel bad.

5 Take regular breaks when you're gaming. Give your eyes, hands, and brain a rest, and get your body moving.

6 Don't download, install, or stream any games without checking with your parents. Pay attention to the age ratings on games—they exist to protect you from content that might upset or disturb you, or that your parents won't be comfortable with you experiencing.

7 If you play mobile games outside, keep aware of your surroundings. Don't play them alone and don't wander around the neighborhood without your friends or family around you.

2024 LEVEL UP

Editor:
Stuart Andrews

Design:
Andrew Sumner

Contributors:
Phoebe Andrews

COVER IMAGES
Fortnite © 2023 Epic Games, Inc. Fortnite and its logo are registered trademarks of Epic Games, Inc. in the USA (Reg. U.S. Pat. & Tm. Off.) and elsewhere. All rights reserved.

Genshin Impact © 2023 miHoYo Co, Ltd. All Rights Reserved.

Mario + Rabbids: Sparks of Fate © 2021, Ubisoft Entertainment. All rights reserved.

Dragon Quest Treasures © 2023 by Armor Project/Bird Studio/ Square Enix. All rights reserved.

Splatoon 3 © 2023 by Nintendo. All rights reserved.

Monster Hunter Rise: Sunbreak © 2023 by Capcom Co., Ltd. All rights reserved.

SpongeBob SquarePants: The Cosmic Shake © 2023 THQ Nordic AB, Sweden. SpongeBob SquarePants © 2023 Viacom International Inc.

Copyright © 2023 by Scholastic Inc. All rights reserved. Published by Scholastic Inc., *Publishers since 1920*. SCHOLASTIC and associated logos are trademarks and/or registered trademarks of Scholastic Inc. No part of this publication may be reproduced, stored in a retrieval system, or transmitted in any form or by any means— electronic, mechanical, photocopying, recording, or otherwise—without written permission of the publisher. For information regarding permission, write to Scholastic Inc., Attention: Permissions Department, 557 Broadway, New York, NY 10012.

The publisher does not have any control over and does not assume any responsibility for author or third-party websites or their content, including the websites of any brands, gamers, and social media personalities included in this book.

ISBN 978-1-339-01249-0
10 9 8 7 6 5 4 3 2 1
23 24 25 26 27
Printed in the U.S.A. 40
First printing, September 2023

CONTENTS

32

36

52

68

92

122

116

134

150

172

184

194

THE BIG GAMES

52 Fortnite

190 Hogwarts Legacy

16 Legend of Zelda: Tears of the Kingdom

78 Sonic Frontiers

56 Genshin Impact

48 Splatoon 3

92 Marvel's Midnight Suns

28 Pokémon Scarlet and Violet

142 Minecraft

Whatever games or types of games you love, we want to help you level up! Read on and get the inside info about the biggest games of the last twelve months—and the games we're most excited about playing next! Along the way, you'll find features that will take you deeper into the world of games, plus pages of hints and tips for the biggest games around. We're here to boost your skills and help you take on every challenge, whether you're playing solo or online!

202 Fire Emblem: Engage

20 Street Fighter 6

158 Disney Dreamlight Valley

7

THE 30

GREATEST GAMING MOMENTS

30

29

GOING OLD-SCHOOL
Sea of Stars

■ Between *Chained Echoes*, the *Eiyuden Chronicle* games, *Live A Live*, and *Octopath Traveler II*, we've had some great retro RPGs in the last year or two. Indie favorite *Sea of Stars* is right up there with the best, giving us a story line straight from classic nineties Japanese RPGs like *Chrono Trigger*, but with a more sophisticated style of pixel art and some brilliant twists in the game play. It's not just about the nostalgia—this is an old-school epic you'll remember for years!

YOUR OWN MAGIC KINGDOM
Disney Dreamlight Valley

■ You might have expected an *Animal Crossing* clone with a Disney makeover, but *Dreamlight Valley* has a bit more substance, putting classic Disney characters at the heart of some ingenious quests. And the more you play it, the more it feels like your own magical place, where you're making friends, solving problems, and putting your own stamp on the world. If there's any place in your heart for Disney and Pixar's movies, *Dreamlight Valley* is going to find it and fill it with a nice warm glow.

28

BRINGING THEM BACK HOME
Kerbal Space Program 2

■ *Kerbal Space Program 2* has lots for you to learn and master, especially if you struggle with the science. Your first attempts to launch a Kerbal into space are almost guaranteed to end in disaster, and you can forget about bringing them safely home. That's why it's such an achievement when you finally pull off a mission, replacing haphazard hilarity with a sense of triumph at a job well done. If the Kerbal astronauts are the heroes, you got them there and back.

27

JOINING FORCES WITH THE MOBS
Minecraft Legends

■ For years we've been cowering away from the Creepers and running scared of the Skeletons and Zombies, but *Minecraft Legends* turns that upside down. In *Legends*, the mobs are on our side, helping to defeat the Piglin invaders, sending them shrieking back to the Nether where they came from. It might take more than one game before we learn to love them, but at least we saw *Minecraft*'s mobs in a whole new light.

OUT OF THE PAGES
The Plucky Squire

26

■ *The Plucky Squire* starts out as a tale from the pages of a storybook, but gets really interesting when the villain kicks the heroic Jot out. Suddenly you're switching between the 2D pages of the living book and the 3D world of the house outside, solving puzzles, blasting bad guys with your jet pack strapped on, and slaying monsters on the building blocks on the bedroom floor. It's the kind of game that loves to play around—and we're happy to let it.

25

IMPOSSIFICATION
Park Beyond

■ Theme park management games are nearly always fun, but *Park Beyond* takes its thrill rides to new heights of terror and excitement. While most rides follow the usual laws of physics, others can be impossified. Build wild coasters where the cars can jump from track to track, or spinning rides that can literally throw thrill-seekers around. And beneath the gimmick, you still have a brilliant, super-absorbing simulation. What's not to love?

24

RIDE 'EM, SPONGEBOB
SpongeBob SquarePants: The Cosmic Shake

■ We're not saying that he's the next Mario, but SpongeBob is making it big as a video game star. The *Battle for Bikini Bottom* remake was a winner, and the *Nickelodeon All-Star Brawl* and *Kart Racers* games were pretty cool. Well, now he has an even better platform game to crow about, and it's packed full of memorable moments. We've struggled to pick just one, but SpongeBob's seahorse-riding Old West antics have to be in the mix.

23

EIGHT-WAY EPIC Octopath Traveler II

■ It's not easy following up one of the most-loved Japanese RPGs of the last decade, but *Octopath Traveler II* is better than the original. One of the complaints about the first game was that the heroes didn't spend much time together and that some stories didn't really link up. Well, the sequel fixes both points in the way that its eight tales and their stars are pulled into a larger story. You're going to have your favorites, but you always want to know what happens next.

22

AIR JORDAN
NBA 2K23

■ Like most sports games, *NBA 2K* is in danger of becoming predictably good. It's getting harder to add new features, while new modes don't always work as well as they should. But if there's one thing that *NBA 2K23* absolutely nails, it's the Jordan Challenge mode. You get to play through fifteen crucial Michael Jordan games, each with three goals to complete. Each comes with vintage uniforms and TV filters to take you right back to the early days. A worthy tribute to a b-ball great.

21

JOINING THE STRAW HAT CREW
One Piece Odyssey

■ There aren't many adaptations of Japanese anime that really capture the look and feel of the real thing, but *One Piece Odyssey* joins *Dragon Ball Z: Kakarot* in doing just that. This grand JRPG adventure with the stars of the Straw Hat Pirates is an absolute blast. Whether you're racing around town as Monkey D. Luffy or brawling with Sanji and Nami, you can see this is a game that understands the characters and what makes them tick.

19

EXPLORING RAINBOW ISLAND
Slime Rancher II

■ You might expect *Slime Rancher II* to play like *Slime Rancher* on a bigger scale, but Rainbow Island and its smiling slimes are an irresistible combination. At first you can only get so far, but the more you discover and the more devices you can unlock and upgrade, the more you find that even distant corners of the island can be reached if you put the time in. What's more, each area is mysterious and beautiful in its own special way. *Slime Rancher II* is a treat to explore.

20

SNAP! Marvel Snap

■ So long, *Legends of Runeterra*, and goodbye to *Hearthstone*— there's a new collectible card game on the block. *Marvel Snap* is an instant all-time great, and not just because of its unbeatable lineup of heroes and villains. It's fast-paced with some ingenious game play ideas, and it's also incredibly accessible. Nothing beats the feeling of when you Snap an opponent while you're winning, except defeating one when they've assumed victory and Snapped!

18

THE OLD GUARD RETURN Fire Emblem Engage

■ Not everyone gets *Fire Emblem*'s long and complicated history—and many players will have started with *Fire Emblem: Three Houses* and *Fire Emblem Warriors: Three Hopes* on the Switch. One of the joys of playing *Fire Emblem: Engage* is that it finds a way to bring back heroes from across the best games in the series, including Byleth from *Three Houses*, Lucina from *Awakening*, and the legendary Marth from the early games. Don't worry—it still has some new heroes to root for, too!

THE COMEBACK CONTINUES
Sonic Frontiers

■ Sonic's output has been spotty for a decade. Even the best Sonic of the last generation, *Sonic Mania*, was a retro tribute to the original Sonic games. *Sonic Frontiers* isn't perfect, but it's fast, packed with action, and full of fresh ideas. Its platform courses are jam-packed with spectacular moments, and it actually has free-roaming worlds that you feel like exploring. If Sega can build on Sonic's finest game in years, then the hedgehog could be back where he belongs.

17

16

DRIVE ANGRY
Need for Speed: Unbound

■ Here's another series that was badly in need of a reboot, and *Need for Speed: Unbound* gave us that and then some. The racing is fast, challenging, and furiously addictive, with cop chases that will keep you on the edge of your seat. There's also time for some awesome stunt challenges, while the mix of realistic cars and scenery with graffiti-style animations makes *Unbound* one of the most exciting-looking games of the year. You'll work for every win and love every minute.

15

HUNTING THE KEMONO
Wild Hearts

■ It's a brave game that takes on *Monster Hunter*, but *Wild Hearts* is more than just a clone. Its focus on mystic powers and homebuilt gadgets adds some new flavors to the normal recipe, while its gigantic Kemono beasts can be terrifying. Most of all, it combines a difficulty level that can make grown men cry with the sense that you're only one small step away from victory. And nothing could be sweeter than bringing down these sky-high varmints and grabbing the reward.

14

THE TERASTAL PHENOMENON
Pokémon Scarlet and Violet

■ *Pokémon Scarlet* and *Pokémon Violet* sometimes felt a little too ambitious for the Switch, but if the action was sometimes jerky, you still had to love the critter-battling game play and the way you felt free to explore sunny Paldea. And in the new Terastal mechanics, it found a fresh way to mix up the big battles, giving familiar Pokémon new Tera Types, perks, and moves that made fighting with them—or against them—even more exciting.

13

MASTERING THE STRAND
Destiny II: Lightfall

■ Each new *Destiny II* expansion has brought weird new worlds to see and powers to wield, but *Lightfall* gave us one of *Destiny*'s best locations in the neon-colored city of Neomuna and some of its most amazing abilities with the Strand. Woven from the threads that hold reality together, your new Strand powers could be twisted into pet monsters, harnessed to teleport through the air, or molded into savage claws. Either way, the Witness and his evil allies are in big trouble and going down!

12

VACATION IN SUMERU Genshin Impact

■ *Genshin* begins with a setting straight out of a million RPGs, but dig deeper and you'll find stunning, exotic regions based on ancient China and Japan. The Sumeru region is another treat, combining the jungles and hill towns of India with the deserts of the Middle East. While the monsters and ancient mechanical guardians make your Sumeru vacation a bit tricky, it's still a top destination for sightseeing, and an even better one for big adventures.

11

BOWSER FTW
Mario + Rabbids: Sparks of Hope

■ Between a new hero, Edge, and some brilliant worlds and villains, there's plenty to love about the *Mario + Rabbids* sequel. All the same, nothing beats having Mario's big bad on your team. Bowser comes packing serious firepower and he's also a hard guy to bring down. Sure, he's not the best team player. He's a bad example to the Rabbids, and he's meaner than he needs to be—but when the chips are down, whose side do you want him on?

10

WHEN IT CLICKS . . .
Overwatch 2

■ When you first start playing the game, *Overwatch 2* seems like it's not worth the hype. Doesn't it feel a lot like the first game, only with some new modes and heroes bundled in? The more you play it, though, the better it gets, and Blizzard's work starts making sense. The updated 5v5 team battles give you more space for strategy and to feel more balanced, while the lineup of heroes and abilities has never looked or played better. It's more *Overwatch* at its best—and that's a wonderful thing!

9

HANGING WITH THE HEROES
Marvel's Midnight Suns

■ Firaxis's action-packed Marvel tactics game shouldn't work half as well as it does, but the real surprise is how much you'll enjoy all the stuff that comes in between the fights. Sure, the battles are brilliant, with their cool, card-based mechanics, but what really gets us is all the social stuff as Marvel's mightiest and darkest heroes learn to get along. Between Blade crushing on Captain Marvel and making friends with Peter Parker, hanging out with superheroes has never been so much fun.

13

8 FIRST ACROSS THE LINE
Forza Motorsport

■ *Gran Turismo 7* gives it serious competition, but *Forza Motorsport* might be the best realistic racer ever made. You can see, feel, and hear the effort that Turn 10 has put into the *Forza* reboot. Playing with a controller, the handling makes you feel the point where the tires start slipping as you speed around a corner, while the engine noise and detailed visuals put you right at the heart of the race. Each event is a thrill and a challenge that always leaves you wanting more.

VR: THE NEXT GENERATION PSVR2 7

■ VR hasn't taken off as quickly as some of us predicted, but we're seeing a new wave of headsets with the potential to turn that around. Meta Quest 2 isn't going anywhere, but Sony's PSVR2 is a real game changer. Combine its crystal-clear 3D displays, smooth motion, and 3D audio with superb controllers and the power of PS5, and you've got a VR system that can run some awesome games. Play *Horizon Call of the Mountain* or *Gran Turismo 7* and you know that you're looking at the future of VR.

5 WIELDING THE SPLATANA
Splatoon 3

■ Third time's a charm for the *Splatoon* series, matching the genius multiplayer with a new setting, a bunch of cool new guns and gadgets, and the series' best single-player campaign. For real *Splatoon* fans, though, it's all about the weapons. Some of us love the new Stringers, some us love the Brushes, but if there's one weapon we all think is awesome, it's the mighty Splatana. Just get in close, charge it up, and slash away!

6 NOT THE LAST JEDI
Star Wars Jedi: Survivor

■ Let's face it—between Luke Skywalker, Ben Kenobi, Grogu, Ahsoka Tano, and *Star Wars Jedi: Fallen Order*'s Cal Kestis, Order 66 didn't do a great job of wiping the Jedi from the *Star Wars* galaxy. Still, it's great to see one of gaming's greatest Jedi back in action. Cal's a more confident figure in the new game, ready to fight with his lightsaber and all the power of the Force. And with weird new worlds and dark new threats to face, he's going to need all that and more.

NEW FRONTIERS
Fortnite Chapter 4

■ By now, *Fortnite* should be running out of steam, but with *Chapter 4* it's just getting started. New graphics have brought it slap-bang into the PS5 and Xbox Series X era, while the revamped island comes crammed with great locations and sneaky secrets, with more arriving with each season. Each new season also brings cool new outfits, not to mention new weapons, gadgets, and mechanics. The result? *Fortnite* still feels fresher than some games that launched a month ago.

TIME FOR SCHOOL Hogwarts Legacy

■ Harry Potter fans have waited years for a game that gives you the full Hogwarts experience, and while the Hogwarts of *Hogwarts Legacy* comes a century before the Hogwarts of the books, it still has all the lessons and locations we've been hoping for. It's also a fantastic adventure, where you have the chance to create and develop your own witch or wizard and defeat dark wizards in the days before Grindelwald, let alone Voldemort. Magical, in all the best ways.

HADOKEN! Street Fighter VI

■ The *Tekken* and *Soulcalibur* games have always been great, but if you want a game that takes the fighting game somewhere new, it always seems to be *Street Fighter*. *Street Fighter II* took the fighting game into the big leagues, while *Street Fighter IV* showed how you could blend wacky characters and comic-book style with spectacular 3D graphics and special effects. Now the sixth game combines a more realistic look with brutal combos, screen-filling special moves, and still a hint of the original's extravagant style. It's big, mighty, and magnificent—and it's going to inspire a new wave of fans.

THE LEGEND RETURNS
Legend of Zelda: Tears of the Kingdom

■ Even before *Breath of the Wild*, a new Zelda was a real event. As a direct sequel to Nintendo's Switch masterpiece, *Tears of the Kingdom* faced even bigger expectations. It meets them not by copying what worked in *Breath of the Wild,* but by taking the game play in a different direction, with new abilities that see Link soaring through the skies above Hyrule, and a story line that's not afraid to look into the shadows and confront the darkness at the heart of the saga. *Breath of the Wild* is often championed as one of the best games ever. *Tears of the Kingdom* might not beat it, but it's worthy of a place beside it. Gaming doesn't get better than this.

Legend of Zelda:
Tears of the Kingdom

The destiny of Hyrule is in your hands!

■ Thought you were done defending Hyrule after defeating Calamity Ganon? Think again. *Legend of Zelda: Tears of the Kingdom* reveals a new threat to Link and Zelda's homeland. An ancient evil has reawakened, spreading its malice. Great chunks of Hyrule—including Hyrule Castle—have been hurled into the sky. The monsters you'd thought you had defeated are back, stronger than before, while terrifying new dangers stand between you and the safety of the realm. This is a job for a hero—and Link's most legendary adventure yet!

Monsters on the rise!

■ Hyrule's Moblins, Bokoblins, Lizalfos, and Stal are back on the warpath again—along with new creatures lurking underground, underwater, and up in the air.

Rock the blocks

■ Colossal bruisers made of stone are nothing new in Hyrule, but these guys are something else! Link's going to have to find their weakness if he wants to bring them down.

New wheels

■ Link can still ride and glide around Hyrule's landscapes, but his new Fuse abilties enable him to construct and drive new vehicles. How do you like the thought of taking this bad boy for a spin?

Reach for the sky

■ When you need to head up into the sky, your old-school glider isn't going to cut it. Luckily, the same Fuse skills that build ground vehicles can also be harnessed for high-speed aircraft.

FAST FACT

With the world over and under Hyrule to explore, *Tears of the Kingdom* is literally the biggest *Legend of Zelda* yet. It takes up over 18 GB on your Switch, against 14.4 GB for *Breath of the Wild*.

Hand of Fate

■ Link's hand has been corrupted, but it has also been blessed with incredible new powers. Ultrahand enables him to lift huge objects and manipulate ancient artifacts, while Recall gives him the power to make objects move backwards in time!

Star Wars Jedi: Survivor

The Jedi order has fallen, but Cal Kestis is fighting back!

■ *Star Wars Jedi: Fallen Order* introduced us to Cal Kestis, the Jedi Padawan who escaped the Order 66 purge and went into hiding on a junkyard planet. We watched Cal rebuild his powers, complete his training, and escape the Imperial Inquisitors. Now, five years on, he's ready for the next step on his journey—to take a stand and fight for his friends and the legacy of the Jedi Knights.

Return of the Jedi

■ Cal is no longer a fugitive Padawan but a full Jedi Knight in control of his powers. All the Force Push, Force Pull, Wall Run, and Jedi Jump abilities are yours to command, and you'll need them to face Imperial Stormtroopers, bounty hunters, and a host of other bad guys.

FAST FACT

Since appearing in *Fallen Order*, Cal Kestis has become part of the *Star Wars* canon, appearing in the novels *Star Wars: Brotherhood* and *Star Wars Jedi: Battle Scars*. *Battle Scars* picks up Cal's story between *Fallen Order* and *Survivor*.

Bring your bestie

■ Cal's Droid companion, BD-1, is back for the ride, and he's every bit as handy as he was in their first adventure. Healing, hovering, and hacking with a Scomp Link are only the start of BD-1's skills, so expect more surprises from the pint-size explorer!

New friends and enemies

■ While you'll see old faces from the first game, Cal has new allies to discover and new enemies to defeat. Cal faces danger from mysterious Imperial figures and has battle droids and bounty hunters on his trail. And who has Cal discovered floating in this bacta tank?

Master of the lightsaber

■ Cal had plenty of time in *Fallen Order* to work on his lightsaber skills, and when it comes to dueling, defense, and throwing his blade, he's a master of the deadly Jedi weapon. He's also getting the chance to upgrade his lightsaber further. How about this Jedi spin on the Kylo Ren crossguard lightsaber?

Get ready to ride

■ Cal has some new skills to show off in *Jedi: Survivor*. For instance, he can make friends with the local wildlife and use them to get around. Massive aerial predators make a handy way to glide around, or you can charge into battle on the back of this long-limbed beast!

STREET FIGHTER 6

THE WORLD WARRIOR RETURNS!

An all-new *Street Fighter* is a big event—and *Street Fighter 6* is the most exciting entry in the series since the mighty *Street Fighter IV* hit fifteen years ago! Not only has Capcom gone for a bold new look, mixing more realistic animation with a gritty comic-book style, but it's mixed up *Street Fighter*'s game play to make it even more incredible!

Combine three brilliant game modes with new control options and a roster of eighteen fearsome fighters, and you have a game that both *Street Fighter* noobs and experts will love. Read on to discover the new champions, the new features, and the amazing new Drive system!

START SIMPLE
■ New to *Street Fighter*? Start off playing Ryu, Luke, or Guile. Their moves and play styles are relatively simple to begin with, and you still get some advanced moves to master.

DON'T OVER-DRIVE
■ Your new Drive moves can be brutally effective, but don't spam them all the time. Using up your Drive Gauge makes you exhausted—which leaves you open to attack.

GO CLASSIC
■ The new control system makes it easy to pull off special moves, but you don't get the full move set. As you get better, practice with the classic controls. It's the only way to beat the best!

HERE COMES A NEW CHALLENGER

■ Ryu, Chun-Li, Dhalsim, and the rest are back, but no new *Street Fighter* would be complete without some new challengers on the roster. Check out these four new champs.

JAMIE
■ Jamie's an expert dancer as well as a Chinatown peacekeeper and master of martial arts. You can see it in his extravagant kicks and acrobatic special moves. This dude loves to show off!

KIMBERLY
■ The latest ninja in the *Street Fighter* series, Kimberly has picked up lots of tricks from her mentor, Guy. Watch out for sneaky, speedy moves—not to mention her classic 1980s street style!

MARISA
■ Marisa combines a career as a jewelry designer with her love of classical Greek culture. Her fighting style is inspired by ancient Greek boxing and wrestling, so expect a painful history lesson.

FAST FACT
Fighting games are known for their strong women, but *Street Fighter*'s Chun-Li was the first, appearing in *Street Fighter II* back in 1991! A massive fan favorite, she's sometimes called "The First Lady of Fighting Games."

JP
■ Johann Pavlovich, JP for short, is the head of a powerful international organization. Don't let his walking cane fool you—he's got a nasty habit of whacking you with it.

THREE MIGHTY MODES

■ *Street Fighter V* got a lot of criticism for not having enough modes at launch. *Street Fighter 6* isn't making the same mistake, packing in three awesome game modes from the start.

FIGHTING GROUND

■ This is where you'll find all the classic *Street Fighter* options, including arcade, online matches, training matches, and local Versus play, for when you just want to battle your buddies, one-on-one.

BATTLE HUB

■ *Street Fighter 6*'s social space, where you can take your avatar for a spin, meet other fans, and kick off a match against them. It's a great place to enter a tournament or just hang out with your friends. You can even try your hand at some classic Capcom arcade games.

WORLD TOUR

■ World Tour is the brand new single-player game mode, where you can create your own *Street Fighter* avatar and take them on a globe-trotting *Street Fighter* master class. You can travel to Metro City, Italy, France, Jamaica, and more, and train with some of the best-loved fighters from the series. Pay attention and you can learn their special moves!

TAKE CONTROL

■ *Street Fighter 6* gives you a choice of three different control modes. Classic is the six-button scheme *Street Fighter* fans know and love, while the Modern system replaces complex combos with simpler one-button commands. You can pull off Ryu's Hadoken move by just pressing the Y or Triangle button. Finally, the Dynamic system makes things even easier.

Just press one of the auto-attack buttons, and the game will pick attacks and combos based on your position!

■ The Modern and Dynamic schemes are great for players that are new to the game, but you can't pull off the full range of your character's moves unless you switch to the Classic mode!

LEARN TO DRIVE

■ The new Drive system is the heart of *Street Fighter 6*'s new fight mechanics. Your Drive Gauge has six bars that you can spend on powerful blocks, attacks, and counters. You can refill it by dishing out attacks and pulling off perfectly timed Punish Counters.

PARRY AND REVERSE

■ Use Drive Parries to block your opponent. It'll cost you half a bar, but time it perfectly and you'll refill it in an instant. Perform a counterattack while blocking and you'll pull off a Drive Reversal, which can help you get out of a situation where your opponent is clobbering you repeatedly.

DRIVE RUSH

■ You can also follow up a Drive Parry with a superpowered rush. It's brilliant for getting you close to your opponent, ready for a high-impact attack. Drive Rush also works from a normal attack, though it will cost you three bars rather than the normal one bar.

DRIVE IMPACT

■ The Drive Impact is a powerful strike that absorbs an incoming attack. You won't feel the hit, and if your opponent is in a corner, they might find themselves going splat against the wall! Ouch, that's gotta hurt!

OVERDRIVE

■ Looking for the most powerful special moves? Press two of the same button type when pulling off a special move and it will be transformed into an Overdrive Art—a spectacular, supercharged attack that should smash your opponent off their feet! Each Overdrive Art costs two Drive Gauge bars.

LIKE THIS? TRY THIS:

MARVEL VS. CAPCOM INFINITE

■ See what happens when the stars of *Street Fighter* meet the world's mightiest Marvel heroes in one massive superpowered brawl. The tag-team battles are amazing!

METROID PRIME REMASTERED

JOIN SAMUS ON HER GREATEST ADVENTURE

It might be twenty years old, but *Metroid Prime* is a classic—and Nintendo has now remade it for a new generation of gamers with *Metroid Prime Remastered* on the Switch. It's the game that took ace intergalactic bounty hunter, Samus Aran, from 2D into 3D, and it's an amazing first-person adventure that hasn't lost any of its impact!

The game sees Samus summoned by a distress signal from a Space Pirate frigate in orbit around the planet Tallon IV. An explosion aboard the ship causes Samus's suit to malfunction, stripping her of her most advanced abilities, yet she lands her ship on the planet, ready to investigate. Can she uncover the secrets of Tallon IV and its ancient civilizations, and regain her powers? You'll need brains, skill, and some alien technology to find out!

QUICK TIPS

SAVE YOURSELF!
■ *Metroid Prime Remastered* has no autosave, so remember to use the Save Stations scattered around the different areas to save the game and restore Samus's energy.

KEEP TRACK
■ Throughout the game, you'll find areas you can't open without a specific weapon or upgrade. Remember where these are—you'll want to come back to them later!

TINY TUNNELS
■ Keep an eye out for small spaces or tunnels that your Morph Ball might squeeze into. They could lead you to a new area or a hidden upgrade.

SURVIVE TALLON IV

■ Samus lands on Tallon IV with only the remains of her armor and her most basic weapons. That's not ideal when the surface is crawling with hostile critters, not to mention the freezing cold and boiling hot environments, ancient traps, and alien threats. How will she make it through?

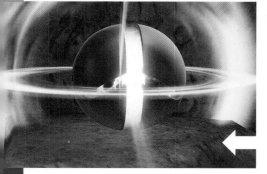

MIGHTY MORPHIN'
■ Get Samus's armor back in shape and she can transform into a critter-crushing Morph Ball, grapple and swing across chasms, or use her jet boots to reach higher spots. You'll need all these abilities and more to explore the planet.

REPAIR AND REEQUIP
■ You can't boss as a bounty hunter without a full set of weapons? Samus's base blaster isn't much better than a peashooter, but get your missiles, charge shots, beams, and bombs going, and you'll be ready for anything!

DEBUGGING
■ Between the giant-sized bugs, killer alien wasps, stabbing tentacles, and tough, spiky varmints, the wildlife of Tallon IV feels like it's out to get you. However, even the toughest critters have a weakness, if you just know where to hit 'em or what to hit 'em with!

MEET THE METROIDS
■ It's not just the local pets that are trying to kill you. Metroids—parasitic, jellyfish-like life-forms—have been let loose on the planet, while the Space Pirates behind the original distress call are also up to no good.

FAST FACT

Kraid, a boss from the older *Metroid* and *Super Metroid* games, was meant to put in an appearance in *Metroid Prime*. Sadly, he was cut for time reasons and didn't feature in another *Metroid* game until *Metroid Dread* in 2021.

LIKE THIS? TRY THIS:

METROID DREAD
■ While it's a return to the original 2D *Metroid* games, *Metroid Dread* is another superb Samus adventure, crammed with thrilling action sequences, mystery, and suspense.

MARVEL'S SPIDER-MAN 2

Twice the web-heads, double the trouble!

What could be even better than Marvel's Spider-Man? We reckon it's one of the greatest—if not *the* greatest—superhero games of all time! Well, how about a sequel starring both Peter Parker and junior Spidey, Miles Morales, and featuring some of the biggest, scariest villains in the whole Marvel Comics pantheon? Well, that's exactly what we're looking at here. Get your web-shooters ready, and prepare for some slinging and swinging!

FIGHT LIKE SPIDEY
■ Peter and Miles have their own moves and styles of combat. Miles can harness his electrical powers to blast and stun, while Peter has the more advanced technology and years of crime-fighting experience behind him. These bad guys have met their match!

WORKING TOGETHER
■ Are two web-heads better than one? Miles and Peter are going to have to work together to handle some of Marvel's most dangerous villains and put a stop to a nefarious plot.

THE BIG APPLE
■ Just like in the first game, you're free to roam around New York City. You'll find plenty of crime to fight on the streets and rooftops, even before you tackle any supervillains.

BIG GAME HUNTER
■ The big V isn't the only predator in town. Kraven the Hunter is out there, looking for the ultimate challenge. Will he find it in our two Spider-Men, or is Venom the foe he's been waiting for?

DEADLY VENOM
■ Who's hiding in the shadows? That man-eating symbiote monster, Venom! What is the creature's purpose, and could he mean the end for not just one, but two, Spider-Men? Prepare for some big surprises!

FAST FACT
This isn't Kraven's first appearance in a Spider-Man game. He made his debut as a boss in the Game Boy Spidey-sequel, *Spider-Man 2: The Sinister Six*, in 2001.

POKÉMON
SCARLET AND VIOLET

THE POKÉMON THAT LETS YOU GO!

I t's time to say a big "Hola!" to a brand new region—and a new way to play *Pokémon*. *Pokémon Sword* and *Shield* experimented with open-world game play, while *Pokémon Legends: Arceus* let you roam freely around its areas, but *Pokémon Scarlet* and *Violet* are the first games in the series where you can go where you want and do what you want in almost any order!

Inspired by Spanish and Portuguese cultures, the Paldea region is a land of wonders, where you can enroll in an elite Pokémon academy and take your first steps toward becoming a Pokémon champ. Yet there's so much more you can do, with three separate story paths to follow and another Pokédex to complete. This could be your biggest *Pokémon* adventure yet!

QUICK TIPS

LET'S GO!
■ Your lead Pokémon doesn't have to stay in its ball—it can travel ahead, fight, and collect items for you. Use the Let's Go! command to level them up faster and gather goodies on the run.

PACKED LUNCH
■ Make sure you've got sandwiches or picnic food if you're going on a dangerous journey. Whatever you eat, you and your Pokémon will end up with some useful perks and buffs.

TAKE ON TRAINERS
■ Too many battles can slow the game down, but by beating other trainers, you can gain experience and money—and you always need plenty of both!

You are challenged by Sergio the Office Worker!

HIT **THE ROAD!**

■ Once you're done with the first prologue section, you can roam around Paldea, heading on or off the beaten track. Instead of set routes, the games have three adventure pathways to follow, where you can learn new techniques, level up, and importantly—catch new Pokémon! You can tackle them in any order, but each pathway will reward you in ways that will make you a better trainer.

VICTORY ROAD

■ This is your traditional *Pokémon* adventure, with eight gym leaders to beat before you can complete the final challenge and call yourself a champion.

Go for it! Beating the gym leaders will push you to build your skills and level up your Pokémon.

FAST FACT

Pokémon Scarlet and *Violet* are the first games in the series where you can tackle the gyms in any order. However, they don't change difficulty with your level, so avoid the tougher gym leaders until you're strong enough to beat them.

> Grunt A
> We're Team Star, kid. We burn so bright, it hurts to look at us! But you knew that, right?

STARFALL STREET

■ Team Star, a group of disruptive students, is causing problems at the academy and blocking students like you from traveling. Track down their five bases and beat the five bosses inside them.

Go for it! Defeat the Team Star bosses to earn League Points and grab powerful new Technical Machines (TMs).

PATH OF LEGENDS

■ Your classmate Arven is a hardcore foodie, and he won't stop until he's collected a bunch of rare herbs. The problem? They're guarded by giant Titan Pokémon. Can you defeat them?

Go for it! Each Titan has a special power that can be learned by your legendary Pokémon, Koraidon or Miraidon. Take on the Titans to power them up!

ENJOY **THE RIDE!**

■ *Pokémon Scarlet* and *Pokémon Violet* each bring one new legendary Pokémon: Koraidon for *Scarlet* and Miraidon for *Violet*. They won't battle for you like other Pokémon, but you can ride them to get from place to place at speed. What's more, you can unlock more abilities for them, enabling them to swim, jump, dash, glide, and climb. With a fully powered legendary on your team, there's almost nowhere you can't reach!

TOTALLY TERASTAL

■ Remember *Pokémon Sword* and *Shield*, with their Dynamax transformations? Well, *Pokémon Scarlet* and *Violet* have something similar with what's called the Terastal phenomenon.

■ Once you've been given your own Tera Orb, you can transform your Pokémon into special Tera forms while they're in battle. Terastalized Pokémon have a tough crystal armor and more powerful moves than their standard moves. They can also have a different type, giving them completely different abilities and weaknesses!

■ It's not just your Pokémon that can turn Tera. You'll encounter Terastalized wild Pokémon that can be battled and captured. They may have different Tera forms than the Pokémon on your team. You can also take part in Tera Raid battles, where you and up to three other players can take on giant Tera Pokémon and catch them. You know you've gotta catch 'em all, right?

SHARE THE JOURNEY

■ *Pokémon* games have had online challenges and raids for a while, but *Pokémon Scarlet* and *Violet* are the first games where two to four players can adventure together through the game. You can explore Paldea, collect Pokémon, and level them up together—though you can't battle the same Pokémon at the same time. However, you can't gang up and complete the adventure pathways together, so there's no ganging up on the gym leaders or Team Star bosses. Shame!

PALDEAN POKÉMON

■ What would a new *Pokémon* game be without new star Pokémon? We've picked out five of our favorites from *Scarlet* and *Violet*.

FIDOUGH
■ Equal parts puppy and pastry, Fidough is one of the cutest Pokémon ever! This Fairy-type critter evolves into the lovable Dachsbun—with the great Charm, Crunch, and Play Rough moves.

LECHONK
■ We love LeChonk because this hog is funny, and because each LeChonk evolves into the sweet-smelling, damage-dealing Oinkologne. Dig those Headbutt and Take Down abilities!

SKELEDIRGE
■ Fuecoco starts off pretty cute but evolves into this Fire/Ghost monster. His Torch Song, Incinerate, and Fire Blast moves can heat up any battle.

GREAVARD
■ This shaggy Ghost-type Pokémon likes to rest underground with just his candle showing, but he's friendlier than he looks. He's got some great Dark, Ghost, and Fairy moves as well!

KLAWF
■ Forgive this Rock-type Pokémon if he's feeling crabby. He's got some cool claw moves to hit opponents with, and some attacks will just bounce off his shell!

LIKE THIS? TRY THIS:

DRAGON QUEST TREASURES
■ *Pokémon* isn't the only series where you can recruit monsters to join you on adventures. *Dragon Quest Treasures* is all about hunting down loot with the aid of adorable Dragon Quest critters.

DESTINY 2: LIGHTFALL

DISCOVER NEPTUNE'S SECRET CITY AND BATTLE THE SHADOW LEGION

The *Destiny 2* saga has nearly reached its end, and *Lightfall* ups the pace as Guardians get ready for the final chapter. This time you and your fireteam buddies are exploring the secret city of Neomuna, which has stayed hidden on the surface of Neptune for centuries. It's not just you that has discovered it. An army of Dark Cabal warriors, led by their ex-emperor, Calus, has attacked the city. Worse, Calus is now a disciple of the Witness—*Destiny*'s ultimate bad guy—and it's all part of his drive to make humanity extinct!

Neomuna's warriors, the Cloud Striders, fight on to defend their city, but they're going to need all the help your Guardians can give them. Armed with new weapons and a brand new set of darkness powers, you're primed to take Calus and his Shadow Legion down!

QUICK TIPS

SWING INTO ACTION

■ The new Strand powers give you more ways to move around. Use your grapple abilities to reach new areas, find sniping spots, or just get out of trouble!

SWITCH YOUR LOADOUTS

■ *Destiny 2* now allows you to have different loadouts based on a subclass, weapons, and armor. Set up different loadouts and different abilities to tackle different environments or enemy factions.

USE THE TANGLES

■ Those glowing green "Tangles" of Strand energy are designed to be combined with your new Strand powers. Try different skills with them to see the effects or—if in doubt—just blast 'em!

STRANDS OF **DARKNESS**

■ The *Beyond Light* expansion gave Guardians its first Darkness power, Stasis. Now *Lightfall* gives us a second to play with, called the Strand. The Strand allows Guardians to create tools and weapons from the psychic threads that hold the universe together. And when you're up against Calus and the Witness, you're going to need to use them all!

WEAVE YOUR LEGEND
■ Each *Destiny 2* class gets its own new Strand subclass. The Hunter Threadrunner gets an awesome rope dart weapon with powerful attacks, both close-up and at long range. The Titan Beserker can weave the Strand into vicious claws, perfect for slicing through the Shadow Legion's forces.

BAD AND BROODING
■ The new Warlock Broodweaver subclass takes a different tack, using the Strand to summon strange creatures and launch a barrage of missiles at their foes. Combine these new abilities with the floating Tangles, and you'll find new ways to turn the powers of the Darkness against itself.

DARK CABAL
■ The Shadow Legion is like no Cabal army that you've ever fought before. Warped by Calus and the Witness, and equipped with technology from the pyramid ships of the Darkness, they're brutally strong, incredibly tough, and powered-up to destroy Neomuna and its protectors.

THE TORMENTORS
■ The Shadow Legion is also aided by a new Destiny enemy, the Tormentors. Creatures of the Darkness, they're huge, monstrous bad guys wielding deadly scythes that can slice through the hardest armor. They can also grab Guardians and drain them of life. Nasty!

FAST FACT

Lightfall is the penultimate (or second to last) *Destiny 2* expansion. The end chapter, *The Final Shape*, is due to arrive in 2024. Will this be the end of *Destiny* or just this story line? We don't know for sure!

LIKE THIS? **TRY THIS:**

HALO: THE MASTER CHIEF COLLECTION
■ Long before *Destiny*, its creators, Bungie, made their name with the original *Halo* games. You'll find them all, plus *Halo 4*, in the Master Chief Collection. It's epic sci-fi action at its best.

Hades II

If Zagreus can escape the Underworld, can his sister stop a Titan?

■ Family is rough in Supergiant Games' world of Greek myth. In *Hades*, our hero, Zagreus, had to escape his dad's infernal dungeon. Now his sister, Melinoë, has to slay their grandfather, the Titan Chronos, before he goes to war with the Olympian gods!

■ Luckily, Melinoë knows a thing or two about fighting. Not only is she skilled with a range of weapons, but she's a witch with the powers of magic at her command. Fans of *Hades* will know it's a tough but fun dungeon crawler, where every death is just another lesson learned. The sequel—like Melinoë—is a chip off the same block!

Big bro

■ Zagreus was the star of the original *Hades*. Son of Hades, god of the Underworld, he fought to escape his father's dark domain. Through many deaths—and the help of the gods of Olympus—he battled his way through and changed the Underworld forever!

Princess of the Underworld

■ Melinoë is the princess of the Underworld and a powerful witch, schooled by the goddess Hecate to battle Chronos—and destroy him. You can spot her by her spectral left arm and by the fact that, just like Zagreus, she has one red eye and one green one.

MELINOË
UNDERWORLD PRINCESS

I've no excuses for my failure, Headmistress. But I swear to you and all the gods above and below, I'll slay the Titan yet!

Aid from the gods!

■ Like Zagreus, Melinoë can win the favor of the gods, including both the gods of the Underworld and the better-known Olympian gods. Expect help from the goddess of vengeance, Nemesis, and Moros, the god of doom, not to mention Melinoë's uncle Zeus and her kindly cousin Apollo.

NEMESIS
RETRIBUTION INCARNATE

I always thought... if I could just train harder than you, she'd reconsider. And give the task to me.

FAST FACT

Hades II is Supergiant's fifth game but the studio's first-ever sequel. The original won more Game of the Year awards than we can count, including at the New York Game Awards, the Game Developers Choice Awards, the Global Industry Game Awards, and the British Academy Games Awards!

The road to revenge

■ Expect to travel the darkest corners of Greek mythology and battle hordes of nightmarish monsters on the way. Inevitably, Melinoë will fall, but when she does she'll return to her chambers, ready to escape and join the fight again! With every try you grow wiser and more powerful, so use what you learn to win!

VR: THE NEXT GENERATION

VR is back, and it's never looked better!

Is virtual reality the ultimate future of gaming? Well, we might not ever see the end of conventional handhelds and consoles, but don't be surprised if you spend more of your gaming time absorbed in virtual worlds. While there's a lot of hype around the idea of a "metaverse"—a kind of internet of connected VR experiences—there's also no denying that VR games can be exciting in a way that normal screen-based games can't match. If you want to feel like you're at the heart of a great adventure, or sitting in the cockpit of a space fighter, or the world's fastest supercar, then VR is about as close as most of us are going to get!

VR HISTORY

■ The basic concepts for VR go back to 1965, when computer scientist Ivan Sutherland presented his vision of an "ultimate display"—a headset that could show the wearer a computer-generated reality that would be impossible to tell from the real deal. Motion tracking through sensors would ensure that the view reflected every movement of the head, so that you could look around a virtual space in the same way that you looked around a room in the

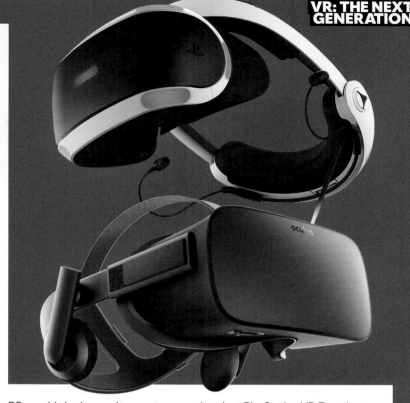

real world. Twenty years later, other scientists such as Jaron Lanier and Thomas Zimmerman at VPL Research began working on more sophisticated VR headsets, and on glove-style controllers that would help you pick things up and interact with them in virtual worlds.

■ In the early 1990s, the first virtual reality arcade games appeared. These huge systems enabled you to sit down, put on a headset, and battle robots and dinosaurs. Or you could fly a World War I biplane or a modern fighter jet. Some companies looked at bringing this technology into the home, to new games consoles or PCs, but low-quality graphics and sky-high prices meant that most never launched. Those that did weren't successful.

■ Things changed around 2010, as VR enthusiasts like Palmer Luckey realized that the powerful 3D graphics hardware found in gaming PCs could also be used to create realistic graphics for a proper VR experience. Luckey designed a headset that became the first Oculus Rift, while other companies, including Google and Samsung, built motion-tracking headsets that worked with a smartphone providing the processing power and the screen. In 2014, Facebook bought Oculus and its technology, while Sony announced its own VR headset, PlayStation VR. Together, the Oculus Rift and PSVR kickstarted a new generation of VR, with games like *Moss*, *Robo Recall*, and *Astro Bot: Rescue Mission* that made the new tech look awesome!

■ The early VR headsets showed that VR could work on PC or console, but many gamers still felt that the technology wasn't quite ready. You had to be tethered to your PC or console with a heavy cable, while the demands of processing different 3D views for each eye meant that you couldn't have the same lavish graphics you might see in other games. The controllers weren't always reliable or accurate, and the headsets soon became hot and uncomfortable in use. But VR technology has kept improving, and we're now looking at a second generation of VR devices. These promise to fix some of the problems of the older VR headsets, and take us to new and even more spectacular virtual reality worlds.

HOW VR WORKS

VR doesn't work by magic. There's some very clever technology behind it.

1 THE DISPLAYS:

At the heart of every VR headset are the displays. You get one per eye to make sure that you get the left and right views you need for realistic 3D vision. Lenses in the headset ensure that each eye can only see that screen, and that the view is sharp and clear.

2 POSITION TRACKING:

The headset will use an external camera or sensors, or a series of built-in cameras, to track your position in the room. So, as you move forward or backward, left or right, or up and down, the views coming through the screen will change to match.

3 MOTION TRACKERS:

The headset also contains a set of motion trackers. These track how and where you move your head, so that as you rotate it left or right, tilt it, or look up and down, the view through the screen will move along with you.

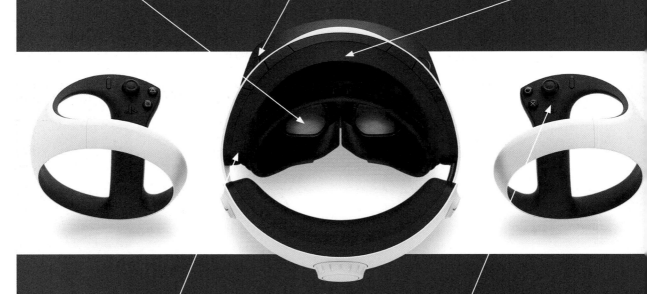

4 3D SOUND:

Your PC or console also takes all this information to track where your ears are, and adjusts the sound coming through the headphones. As such, sounds coming from the left , in front, the right, or behind will appear to come from that direction. Sound plays a really important role in creating a convincing VR experience.

5 CONTROLLERS:

Today's VR controllers combine a mix of conventional analog sticks, buttons, and triggers with motion controls. These enable you to interact with virtual objects in the virtual world, or use a virtual sword, bow and arrow, or other gadget in the way that you might use it in the real world—by aiming it, swinging it, or shooting. Most will also have built-in rumble motors, to deliver a greater sense that you're interacting with real objects, even though they don't exist.

VR SYSTEMS

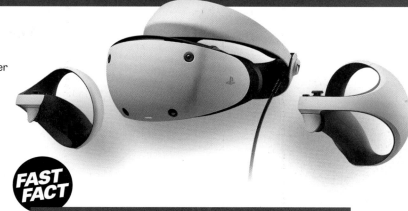

PSVR2

■ Sony's PlayStation VR2 is a massive upgrade over the first-generation headset. For one thing, it has the power of PS5 behind it. For another, its twin 2000 x 2400 pixel OLED displays deliver the brightest, sharpest 4K VR graphics you've seen yet, with silky-smooth 120 frames-per-second movement and HDR. PSVR2 also includes eye tracking, where the headset follows exactly what you're looking at to make sure it's detailed and in focus, along with 3D audio. Meanwhile, vibration feedback in the headset and the new VR2 Sense controller make you feel even more like you're really there. When laser beams are flying past your head, or you pull back on your bow and release an arrow, you can actually feel it!

FAST FACT

Jaron Lanier's EyePhone 1 was one of the first VR headsets, developed and released in 1987. It inspired the movie *The Lawnmower Man* and even starred in it, but it never sold in any big numbers—probably because it cost nearly $15,000!

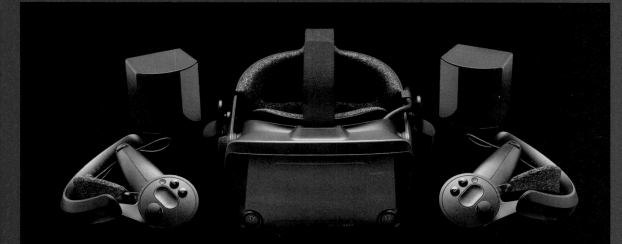

VALVE INDEX

■ The company behind Steam, the Steam Deck, *Half-Life*, and *Dota 2* released its own VR headset back in 2019, and it's still one of the best for PC users. You get an excellent pair of 1440 x 1600-pixel resolution screens and a smooth 120 fps refresh rate, which should stop you feeling ill when playing fast-paced action games.

You also get a wider field of view to look at, along with the most accurate head tracking and the best controllers in VR. Often called the knuckles, these can track the pressure of each individual finger on the grip. The only problem is that it's very expensive—and you'll need an even more expensive PC to make it work.

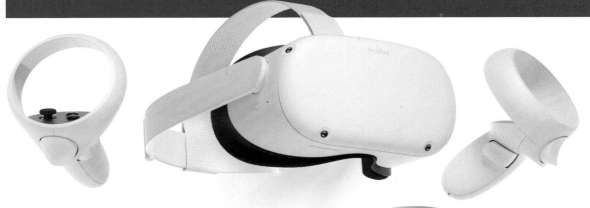

META QUEST 2 AND META QUEST PRO

■ The Meta Quest 2 is getting on a bit, but it's still one of the most versatile VR headsets. You can play VR games using the headset's built-in hardware, or connect it to a PC and play the latest PC VR games. The graphics aren't as sharp or detailed as on PSVR2, but some of the games and experiences are still brilliant, and it's an easier VR headset to just get playing with or use with family and friends. The Meta Quest Pro takes things up another level, with a lighter "ski goggles" design, more computing power, and a new optical system for brighter, clearer visuals. Sadly, it's designed for business rather than gaming, and costs around $1,500!

VR SHOWCASE

HORIZON VR: CALL OF THE MOUNTAIN
(PSVR2)

Sony's biggest PSVR2 game is an offshoot of the awesome *Horizon* series, taking you back to a world of warring tribes and giant robot dinosaurs, only this time it's you, not Aloy, in the middle of the action. Once you've fired off arrows at Watchers and Stormbirds and climbed up mountain sides, handhold by handhold, you'll be hooked!

NO MAN'S SKY (PSVR2, PC)

This epic space exploration game is even better in VR, and the PSVR2 and PC versions do the game's complex galaxies justice. If you've ever wanted to explore strange new worlds or battle pirate fighters in the stars, *No Man's Sky* can make your dreams come true. No other VR game gives you so much freedom or so much to see and do.

GHOSTBUSTERS VR: RISE OF THE GHOST LORD (Meta Quest, PSVR2)

Is there something strange in your neighborhood? Pull on your jumpsuit and your proton pack and sort it out. This VR take on the classic movie franchise sees you opening up a new ghostbusting office in San Francisco, and it's not long before the spooks crawl out from below the streets to give your gang some serious scares. Luckily, this is a co-op adventure. Work together, trap the specters, and you might survive the night!

HELLO NEIGHBOR: SEARCH AND RESCUE (Meta Quest, PSVR2, PC)

What's creepier than everyone's favorite hide-and-seek thriller? How about *Hello Neighbor* in VR. With *Search and Rescue*, it's time to sneak into your neighbor's house and save your friend. The VR experience makes it even more immersive, so you can almost feel every creaking stair and clinking door. Featuring clever puzzles combining multiple characters, it's a game that needs brains as well as nerves of steel.

MOSS: BOOK II (Meta Quest, PC, PSVR2)

The original *Moss* was a highlight of the PSVR library, giving you a brilliant 3D platform game full of puzzles and swashbuckling swordplay, where you could interact with the beautiful scenery to help your tiny mouse hero win the day. *Moss: Book II* is even better, and it looks a treat on PSVR2 and Meta Quest 2.

OVERWATCH 2

Get the hero info and the tips you need to triumph

Overwatch 2 isn't massively different from Overwatch, but that doesn't mean there aren't new heroes, maps, and strategies. What's more, you might be new to Blizzard's mighty hero shooter and in need of some help to be a better player. Either way, we have tips for winning in all four regular match types and advice on playing the sequel's new heroes.

1

2

Start simple

■ If you're an Overwatch noob, start out with simple, straightforward heroes like Soldier: 76, Reinhardt, and Mercy. They're tough and have abilities that don't take a lot of practice to be useful. Play matches against the AI at Casual difficulty settings to get a feel for the maps and modes. That way, when you start joining real matches, you'll be a better player for your team.

Keep changing heroes

■ Struggling to make any impact on the match? Try switching heroes. You can change every time you die, and a new hero can put you right back in the game. Try to work out what your team is missing, or which heroes might counter a power player on the other team. If you've joined the queue in a specific role, though, you'll have to pick another hero of the same type.

FAST FACT

It took eight months for the original Overwatch to build a fanbase of over 25 million players. Overwatch 2 managed it in just ten days, and hit 35 million in the first month!

Play the objective

3

■ Each match type has its own objectives, and completing these is more important than pushing up your kill/death ratio. Make sure you understand what you have to do and the order you have to do it in, then try to be in the right place at the right time to make that happen.

Know the roles

4

■ You need to understand the three roles and how to play them. Tanks guard more vulnerable damage and support characters, blocking and soaking up incoming fire and smashing through the damage characters. Damage heroes are there to do as much damage as they can to the enemy team, while support characters are there to heal and buff their teammates. Every hero has some lethal weaponry, but play your role if you want the team to win.

Capture and control

■ In Control matches you need to work together. Control points are captured or recaptured faster if you have three players from your team inside them, but adding more players than that makes no difference. Once you own the control point, take up defensive positions around it. If you're all standing close together, you can be taken out by a single fierce attack!

5

Play Kiriko

■ Kiriko is one epic support hero. She's fast, she can teleport and climb up walls, and her Kunai blades can dish out some damage if you aim for headshots. Best of all, she can throw projectiles that heal and protect her teammates, while her Ultimate boosts movement and attack speeds. Use her speed to get her where she's needed quickly, then get out safely to do it all over again.

Play Junker Queen

■ Junker Queen is an awesome tank, dishing out impressive amounts of damage with her Jagged Blade and Scattergun, then using her Commanding Shout to buff movement and restore HP. Think of her less as a standard tank, and more as a cool damage/support hybrid.

6

No "I" in team

■ You don't have to stick with the team at all times, but it helps if you play together. If you're a sniper, support your team from a distance and aim for the most threatening foes. If you're a close-up damage dealer, don't just sprint toward the enemy the moment you respawn—regroup with your team and head into battle together. And if your team isn't using voice chat, remember you can use pings to communicate and work better together.

7

Killer combos

■ Some hero combos just work well together. Use Ana's Nano Boost Ultimate with Solder: 76's Tactical Visor and you've got some high damage output that doesn't miss, plus Soldier: 76 can heal his partner if he needs to. Similarly, Junker Queen can be a brilliant tank if she has Brigitte at her side to heal her. Mercy and D.Va can also be awesome, with Mercy buffing D.Va's damage. Try on different combos for size!

Play Sojourn

■ With her Railgun, Power Slide, and Disruptor Shot, Sojourn is great for fast, hard-hitting attacks. Charge up your Railgun, use the Disruptor Shot to take the enemy off-balance, and you're good to attack then slide away when you take too much damage.

Keep pushing

■ Playing Push? Remember that someone has to stick with the robot. It will only keep moving through the level if it has someone with it, and if that someone isn't you, then it might be someone from the other team. Even better, the robot is great for cover, soaking up a whole bunch of gunfire and damage—especially when it's pushing a barricade!

Escort and support

■ Support heroes are even more important in Escort missions. Tanks and damage dealers can defend or attack the payload, but they'll do it a lot better with buffs and healing on their side. If you're playing support, keep doing your job, but if you aren't, then attack the enemy team's support heroes. This will weaken the attackers or defenders and make it easier for your team to destroy them!

Go Hybrid

■ Hybrid matches start off like a Control match but turn into something that's more like an Escort match. When that happens, you need to adapt your tactics quickly and work to either defend or halt the payload. Too many teams lose focus on the new objective, letting the other team reach the goal faster.

Play Ramattra

■ Is he a good guy or bad guy? Who cares? He's another top-tier tank with two forms, each with their own abilities. In one he can pull down flying heroes and create barriers, but in the other he's almost a damage hero, with abilities that should strike fear into the hearts of his opponents. Play defensive until your enemies look weak, then pounce and hit them where it hurts!

45

THE FINALS

The year's hottest online FPS?

It might not have the big brand hype of *Overwatch* or *Call of Duty*, but *The Finals* could be the most exciting online FPS in years. In it, teams of three battle it out in a huge combat game show, eliminating the competition across a series of tournament rounds in the hope that, this time, they could reach the finals. From its masked champions to the way that losing players collapse into a pile of coins, this is one stylish action game. Yet the secret sauce that makes it taste even better is its spectacular destructible environments. Walls, floors, furniture, and ceilings can all be smashed, blasted, and blown away—opening up a whole new range of tactics!

■ The combat is designed to be fast-paced, so you need to be quick on the draw. In a game where almost everything can be obliterated, there's no safe place to hide. The teams that work together are the teams that survive and reach the final round.

■ Destruction is the name of the game. The team at Embark Studios has created tech that enables walls and floors to be blown apart, scenery to be shattered, and whole buildings to collapse. This transforms the way you play—and pumps up the thrill factor to dangerous levels.

■The game's arenas go for a realistic look inspired by European cities. It would be nice to take a stroll and enjoy the scenery—but there's no time to sightsee in this chaos!

■The Contestants in *The Finals* are yours to customize, with different weapon loadouts, looks, and accessories you can use to make them your own. Are you going to go light and sneaky like a ninja, or go for the big guns and try to win through firepower?

■*The Finals* goes big on player creativity. If you think you can do something, try it! Have you got an enemy hiding behind cover? Blast the cover away. Sniper lurking on the rooftop? Take out the roof and bring them down to your level.

FAST FACT

The Finals isn't the first game with destructible scenery. It first became a feature in the classic 2008 FPS *Battlefield: Bad Company*. Key developers from Embark Studios actually worked on that game, so you could say that they're finishing what they started!

47

SPLATOON 3

Top tips to help you win in *Splatoon 3*'s multiplayer modes

S ome people think *Splatoon 3* is just for little kids, but it's as smart, sophisticated, and strategic as any *Overwatch* or *Halo*. It's not hard to find yourself on the winning side from time to time, but if you want to keep on winning, you'll need skill, a knowledge of the modes, maps, and weapons, and some idea of how to play as a team. Struggling with any of that? We've got some helpful ideas.

1 Practice with motion controls

■ Traditional "right stick to aim" controls will get you so far, but *Splatoon 3*'s motion controls can help you get your sights on an Inkling faster —and improve your accuracy. Don't use them for the first time in a live match, but get used to them in Story Mode and Recon Mode. It might take you a while, but you'll be glad you did!

2 Ink around the spawn points

■ Playing Turf War? Before you head off and try to splat the enemy team, cover the area around your spawn point. The more floor you fill with paint, the faster you can travel in squid form through it. More importantly, in a close match every square inch of floor counts. If you're leaving areas around your spawn point empty, you're throwing away percentage points that are rightfully yours!

Master the squid moves

3

■ You're not some slow-moving human running around the map on two legs—you're an Inkling (unless you're an Octoling) and you've got faster ways to get around. Use your squid form in inked-up areas to move around faster, and use the Squid Surge and Squid Roll moves. For the Surge, speed up a wall, stop, then hold the B button until you flash. Let go for a huge launch upward. For the Roll, swim fast through the ink, then switch directions fast as you jump with B. You'll leap across the floor—and you'll be invulnerable while you do it!

4

Splatted Alex!
Splatted CRISPVHAM!

Go for ink and survival over splats

■ You'd think your goals in Turf War mode were obvious—the team that marks the most "turf" in the map with ink wins the match. Yet loads of players will go for splats (or kills) over spreading their ink, even taking silly risks that get them splatted. While you're splatted, you're not laying ink down, so this makes no sense at all. Focus on inking and pushing back on the enemy team while they're inking, and you'll have a better chance of winning.

Stringers for winners

■ *Splatoon*'s new bow weapons are some of the most challenging in the game—but they're great if you can get them right. Learn how aiming and charging work. A quick tap of the trigger will give you a quick burst of ink, but even at close range it's weak. Hold longer for a midrange shot that goes farther and does more damage. Hold for even longer, then release for maximum range and maximum splatting power.

■ Get used to the arc that ink from the stringer follows, and you'll also do a better job of hitting enemy players. You can even hit them when they're hiding behind cover! You can also use explosive shots to boost your damage or your ink coverage farther.

5

Play through Story Mode

■ You should play through the Story Mode, anyway, as it's the best one the series has ever had. You'll meet the Squid Sisters and Splatville's new idols, Deep Cut—it's a spectacular adventure. But you'll also get to grips with all the moves, weapons, gadgets, and specials in *Splatoon 3*, and you can earn a bunch of stuff that you can use to upgrade your gear in multiplayer. Only a fool would miss it!

Stay aware

■ Some weapons and specials give you plenty of warning before you hit, so look out for the indicators and get out of the line of fire. Don't stick around, either, when hard-hitting specials are active. If someone's just started up a Crab Tank or is running around with the Trizooka, keep away! Why help them rack up easy kills?

6

Match your weapons to your role

■ As with most competitive shooters, high-level *Splatoon* players take on one of three roles. Slayers distract enemy players from their objectives and do their best to splat them. They use high-damage weapons or weapons that work up close over a large area.

■ Anchors stick near the starting position and defend from a distance, using long-range chargers and stringers to ink and splat their foes. Supports work in between, keeping the ground inked, providing buffs to the slayers, and helping push into enemy territory. Rollers, Brellas, Brushes, and bombs are ideal! Pick a role, then pick appropriate weapons and specials.

FAST FACT

Turf War doesn't score you for the ink you put on the walls, only the ink that splats across the floor. Inking the walls is still useful for moving and surging, but ink the floor if you want to win!

8

Revenge gets you nowhere

■ Have you been splatted? Using your super-jump to get straight into the action—or get revenge—is a classic rookie mistake. Enemy players will see you coming and go for another splatting. Instead, look for a good space to jump into where you can lay down some paint or hit the other team from a different angle. You'll survive for longer and make a difference to the final score!

Charge and fire

9

■ Charger weapons are amazing at long-distance, but they take a bit of practice to master. Work on getting a feel for how long each one takes to charge up and any cooldown time between shots. Practice your aim so that you're firing as soon as the weapon charges—and you hit every time. Remember that chargers without a scope can hold their charge even while you're swimming, which makes them useful for quick hit-and-run attacks. You lose this with scoped chargers, but they're even better for sniping from long-range!

Winning Anarchy Battle

■ Turf War isn't the only way to play *Splatoon 3*. Want to be a champ? You need to master all four Anarchy Battle modes.

Rainmaker

■ Rainmaker is your classic capture-the-flag mode with a twist. Grab the Rainmaker from the center, then take it to your opponent's base to win. If it's protected by a shield, then you've got a long way to take it before you can score. Activating the checkpoints along the way means that you don't have to start again if you drop the Rainmaker. Focus on the objective and push forward as a team.

Clam Blitz

■ This should be simple. Just collect the clams and throw them in the enemy's basket. Only, the basket is guarded by a shield, and you need to collect eight normal clams to make a power clam that can remove it. Defend players with a power clam and get ready to follow them with your clam collection—and make sure the enemy team doesn't get a chance to use their power clam on you!

Splat Zones

■ Splat Zones is all about capturing control points, or "zones," by covering them in ink. Your aim is to capture all the zones, then hold them. Don't waste time splatting enemy players unless they're in a zone that you're attacking, or closing in on a zone that you're defending. Concentrate on covering the zone with ink!

Tower Control

■ Here the two teams battle for control of a central tower that makes it through the map on a track. The longer you control it, the farther it moves toward the finish mark on the opposing team's side. If you're on the tower, keep moving and use the pole in the middle for cover. Your teammates should be working hard to keep the other team from getting up there to splat you!

FORTNITE

ANOTHER GREAT YEAR FOR BATTLE ROYALE G.O.A.T.

Fortnite is the gaming phenomenon that just won't quit! Six years after it launched, the world's best battle royale is still going strong with its best chapter yet. New gear and tweaks to the core game mechanics have made it even more fun to play, while switching to a new graphics engine has kept it one of the best-looking games around. Fortnite still gets the guest stars and high-profile crossover events that other games can only dream of, and it's still the hub of a thriving creative community producing genius new modes and levels. And do you know what? We reckon the best is yet to come!

QUICK TIPS

STICK THE LANDING
■ Don't jump out too early. Leaving later will often mean landing in a quieter spot where you can stock up on guns, shields, and gadgets before you have to start dodging bullets.

USE YOUR EARS
■ Sound can give you the edge in Fortnite, so put on some headphones and listen. You can track footsteps, listen for gunfire, and hear the hum of a nearby chest.

WARM UP
■ Team Rumble games are great for warming up, especially when the map has changed, or new guns and gadgets have been introduced. You'll get plenty of action and a chance to try things out.

FANTASTIC FOUR

■ *Chapter 4* has put the awe back in *Fortnite*! New tech makes the most of the power of the Xbox Series and PlayStation 5 consoles, while new features have brought new life to the game.

BELIEVE YOUR EYES
■ *Fortnite* now uses Epic's Unreal Engine 5, which has a bunch of brilliant features that allow Epic to build more detailed worlds with lavish lighting and accurate shadows, plus incredible visual effects.

LOOKING GOOD

REFORGED!
■ The Fracture event at the end of *Chapter 3* saw the island destroyed by the Herald then rebuilt from the wreckage by the players and the Paradigm. *Fortnite's* world never stops changing!

FAST FACT

IT'S HAMMER TIME
■ Love it or hate it, the Shockwave Hammer is a real ground-shaker. You can use it to bounce huge distances or smash your foes, and it's always a blast to use.

Over 400 million people have played *Fortnite*, and the game still gets over 3 million players online at the same time— and more for the big events!

THRASH METAL
■ The new vehicles and gadgets keep on coming! *Chapter 4* introduced the Trail Thrasher dirt bike— the perfect vehicle for mad tricks and high-speed racing with the storm at your back!

...NG
...!

...nite's
...ts are never
...oring, and *Chapter 3*
and *Chapter 4* have
given us some
of the craziest
crossovers yet!

GOING ANIME
■ *Fortnite*'s anime-themed outfits always look awesome, whether you stick to homegrown heroes like Nezumi or cosplay as the stars of *Dragon Ball Z*.

CROSSING THE SPIDER-VERSE
■ Spider-Gwen from Marvel's *Spider-Verse* movies is no stranger to switching universes. She's a natural in the world of *Fortnite*, even if there's no wall-crawling going on.

SLAYING IT
■ *Doom*'s Slayer is one of gaming's most iconic heroes, and who's better suited to blasting his way through a lobby's worth of players?

MASTER THE MOVES

■ *Fortnite*'s movement mechanics have evolved since the days of *Chapter 2*. First, Epic introduced sliding. Sprint forward, then hit the crouch button and your hero will slide on the ground. It's great for getting downhill fast and you'll kick objects and other players on impact. Try it for your next dramatic entrance.

■ You can also jump and mantle up ledges or vault over low walls at speed, or use wall-jump and double-jump parkour tricks to dodge gunfire and hit the high spots faster.

CREATION STATION

■ Few games give creators the tools and freedom to create their own modes and games as much as *Fortnite* does. That's why you'll still find awesome maps and modes appearing in the game with every month. We've picked out a few of our favorites.

MOTORCROSS MADNESS DEATHRUN

Island code: 1315-1148-0003

■ *Fortnite*'s Trail-Thrasher dirt bikes are brilliant fun, and they're the star of this spectacular deathrun. Steer, jump, and stunt your way through 30 levels of daredevil biking.

CHAOS COLOR SWITCH

Island code: 9510-5510-7139

■ You know those puzzle games where you have to stand on the tile of the right color or fall to your doom? Well, this is the same thing in vehicles. Jump in a truck and enjoy the car-nage!

LIKE THIS? TRY THIS:

APEX LEGENDS

■ With its amazing lineup of Legends and the best movement and gunplay in the business, *Apex Legends* has to be *Fortnite*'s biggest rival for the battle royale throne. Play it. It's amazing!

KLOMBO VS HUNTERS   Island code: 6670-8009-3580

■ We love a straight two-team deathmatch as much as anyone, but this one comes with a great map surrounded by adorable Klombos. Jump in and show the world your shooting skills.

GENSHIN IMPACT

NEW HEROES, NEW LANDS TO EXPLORE

Genshin Impact is now a phenomenon, played by tens of millions around the world, and it keeps getting bigger and better. Each year sees new heroes introduced to the game, along with new lands, new quests, and a whole new story line. And you can still enjoy it all without spending a dime!

With the nation of Sumeru opening up for business in 2022, and Fontaine and Natlan joining it in 2023 and 2024, the world of Genshin Impact is vast. The tale of the Traveler, the Fatui, and their fiendish Abyss Order is also becoming more epic. The game's complex systems and odd way of doing things can make it an intimidating prospect, but if you want a big adventure full of monsters, gorgeous scenery, and humor, you'll find it here. Don't wait any longer—jump in!

QUICK TIPS

FOOD EQUALS HEALTH
■ Food isn't the only way to restore your health, but it can be the quickest and easiest. Don't head out to battle monsters without a backpack full of meals and snacks.

Stop

EQUIP YOUR ARTIFACTS
■ Keep swapping and enhancing weapons, but don't forget your artifacts. These provide protection and perks for your heroes, and can be enhanced for added bonuses or destroyed for the game's currency, Mora.

MAKE OFFERINGS
■ Each region has its own oculi, whether it's the Aneomoculi in Mondstadt or the Dendroculi in Sumeru. Collect them and offer them at the Statues of the Seven for a Stamina boost and more rewards.

EXPLORE SUMERU

■ Sumeru is a land of lush jungles, mighty rivers, and scorching deserts, where strange ruins hide ancient perils and the ruling Akademiya appears to have its own suspicious secret plans.

THE DIVINE TREE

■ Head to Avidya Forest to find Sumeru City, the capital of the region. Built on the Divine Tree, sacred to the locals, it's the main base of the Sumeru Akademiya and home of the Sanctuary of Surasthana.

Kemia
Researcher
The more imbeciles we take in, the more stupid things we'll deal with every day. It threatens our efficiency. I don't know what's on their mind.

⊡ Start Auto-Play

Lv. 30

RESEARCHERS, RANGERS, AND MERCS

■ Teams of Akademiya researchers roam the jungles and deserts of Sumeru, hoping to uncover the secrets of an ancient culture and its tech. They're protected by mercenaries, but are their activities dangerous? The brave Forest Rangers seem to think so!

MECHANICAL MONSTERS

■ The wilds of Sumeru are crawling with hostile critters and all-around bad guys, from ferocious fungi like the Jadeplume Terrorshroom to Abyss Automatons like the brutally tough Ruin Gargoyle.

FAST FACT

Have you noticed that the animation you see before you enter the game changes according to the time of day in the real world? The sky and the colors change for sunrise, morning, afternoon, and night.

BEAUTY AND DANGER

■ With its mountain gardens and distinctive fruit and flowers, there's plenty to gawk at in Sumeru, but keep your wits about you: great dangers dwell in the jungle and in secret lairs beneath the ground.

Electro-Charged

Tobias

Lisa

Kaeya

FREE WISHES

■ If you want to have the best characters or weapons in *Genshin Impact*, then you're going to have to make a lot of wishes. To do that, you'll have to spend Fate on the banners in the Wishes menu, but both Acquaint and Intertwined Fate can be hard to come by. You can buy either with Primogems, a currency that you can earn in-game, or buy them with real money by way of Genesis Crystals. Before you spend a cent, make sure you check out ways to earn Primogems for free!

Character Event Wish

Reign of Serenity

Probability increased!

Every 10 wishes is guaranteed to include at least one 4-star or higher item.

5-star event-exclusive characters can only be obtained in the specified wish during the specified time period(s). View Details for more.

Time Remaining:
8 day(s) 3 hour(s) 57 minute(s)

Raiden Shogun ★★★★★ UP!
Plane of Euthymia

■ The easiest way is by taking on the four daily commissions. Complete all four and report back to Katheryne at the Adventurer's Guild. She'll give you ten Primogems per commission plus a bonus twenty! You can earn them for completing story quests or Archon chapters, mission objectives in your Adventurer's Handbook, opening chests, and unlocking new teleport waypoints, too. Taking new heroes for a Test Run challenge can also net you loads of Primogems in no time at all!

TOP-TIER HEROES

NILOU
■ Don't dismiss her just because she's a dancer! Nilou wields a Hydro Sword like a top-tier warrior, with some powerful Bloom reactions and awesome elemental skills. Her deadly dance moves mean she's always putting on a show.

CANDACE
■ Candace combines a shield and polearm weapon to either fight aggressively or provide support. With her Element Burst she can boost damage for Hydro-heavy heroes, making her a top team member even if she spends most of her time off the field!

WANDERER
■ Remember Scaramouche from Chapter II of the Archon's quest? He's back in the guise of Wanderer. He can dish out huge amounts of damage through elemental skills, but also buff his teammates while he battles. Useful.

CYNO
■ General Mahamatra of the Akademiya, Cyno is a powerful damage-dealer with some electrifying special moves. Use his electro-polearm to tackle the toughest enemies, with short cooldowns to end the fight faster.

FIGHTING FIT

■ *Genshin Impact* has its share of brutal bad guys, and taking them down can be a big ask. Get to grips with its combat systems, though, and you can take on the hardest mobs!

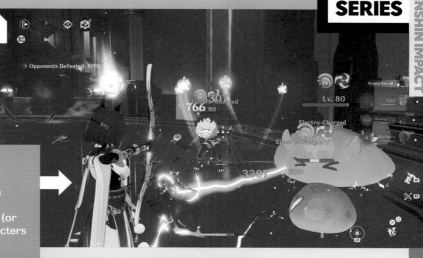

USE THE ELEMENTS
■ Each hero can do damage of a specific elemental type, and this in itself has an effect on battle. Pyro characters can burn their targets (or wooden shields) while Cryo characters can slow or freeze their enemies.

JOIN FORCES
■ You can amplify elemental effects by combining elemental attacks or conditions. Get your foes wet and then electrify them, or use Hydro and Pyro to vaporize them. Each combination has its own cool uses.

CHARGE 'EM UP
■ Getting stomped by charging monsters? Let them charge, dodge their attacks, then come in behind them and hit them hard until they turn. It's a good way to deal with the bigger bruisers, and even better when they're charging with a shield.

DEAL WITH SHIELDS
■ Some monsters come with wooden shields that can be burned, while the Abyss Mages have magical shields that need to be worn down. Luckily, each shield is vulnerable to the opposite element, so use the right hero and ability to break it down!

TIGHNARI
■ One of Genshin Impact's best archer heroes, with arrows that cause bonus Dendro Damage and an Element Burst that fires out tanglevine shafts to hit six enemies at once! He's a good pick for any Sumeru exploration team.

LIKE THIS? TRY THIS:

HONKAI: STAR RAIL
■ *Honkai: Star Rail* comes from the same HoYoVerse stable as *Genshin Impact*, but mixes things up with a sci-fi setting and strategy-based combat. We reckon it's another winner!

GO FREE 2 PLAY

VALORANT

You don't need to pay big bucks to play great games these days, but watch out for the hidden costs!

You've probably noticed that games aren't getting any cheaper. The big exclusives from Microsoft and Sony can cost up to $70, while more and more games now sell for $50 to $60. You can save some cash by buying in sales or going for cheaper indie titles, but gaming is becoming an expensive hobby—and it's hitting us gamers where it hurts!

Luckily, there is an alternative. Games like *Fortnite*, *League of Legends*, and *Apex Legends* have paved the way for "Free 2 Play" games: games that don't cost anything to buy or play, but with the game-makers making money through in-game purchases for characters, cosmetics, and extra content to play through. This used to be associated with games that included dodgy mechanics that forced you to pay for resources that could take weeks to grind for, or games designed to be so addictive that players ended up spending so much on new characters and costumes that they might as well have bought a full-priced game! However, *Fortnite*, *League*, *Apex*, and the games that have followed have gone easy on that kind of thing. While you might be tempted to spend out on cool characters and outfits, you can have fun without giving up a single cent!

We've picked out some of our favorite Free 2 Play games in every style, so that you can give them a go. What's more, you'll find some useful tips to help you avoid spending real-world cash when you really don't have to!

FREE 2 PLAY ACTION

FORTNITE

APEX LEGENDS

■ *Fortnite* is still the king of free battle royale games, and with a new island, new weapons, and new graphics technology, it's never looked or played so good! *Apex Legends* has even better combat, though, and some of the best-designed characters in games. Each season brings new heroes with their own awesome abilities that turn the game's tactics upside down!

■ The competition for the top free hero shooters is also heating up. *Valorant's* focus on skills and strategy has made it a favorite with competitive gamers, but *Overwatch 2* has now gone Free 2 Play, and it's still a great-looking and hugely addictive effort. And if you'd rather battle without heroes and abilities, you can go for *Halo Infinite* multiplayer or the brilliant *Splitgate*. Or why not try the base game of *Destiny II* and become a legendary guardian. All can be downloaded and played, free of charge!

FREE 2 PLAY MOBAS

SMITE

LEAGUE OF LEGENDS

■ *League of Legends* and *Dota 2* did a lot to help build the Free 2 Play scene, and both are still massively exciting multiplayer online battle arena games with a vast roster of heroes and villains to play as and some of the deepest, smartest game play around. *Smite* is another good option. It's a bit more accessible to players with a lower skill level, and you can play it on Switch, PS4, or Xbox One, not to mention PS5 and Xbox Series S/X.

■ New MOBA players might also want to check out *Pokémon Unite*, the Nintendo Switch MOBA that ditches all the muscle-bound warriors and sorcerers of *League* and *Dota 2* for your favorite Pokémon. New critters and seasonal battle passes keep it fresh, and it's also available for Android smartphones, iPhones, and iPads.

FREE 2 PLAY ADVENTURE

TOWER OF FANTASY

■ RPG adventures don't get bigger or more ambitious than the glorious *Genshin Impact*, with a vast fantasy world full of wilderness, dungeons, and bustling cities that expands even more each year. If you're happier with sci-fi than swords, spells, and dragons, then check out *Tower of Fantasy*, an anime-inspired futuristic take on the same basic game play.

■ Capcom's *Monster Hunter* series sets the standard for monster-fighting action RPGs, but *Dauntless* is a great free alternative with great co-op game play, fast-paced combat, and some stunning creatures to battle and landscapes to explore. Meanwhile, *RuneScape* remains one of the most popular massive multiplayer games for a reason. It's easy to get into, but surprisingly deep, with brilliant story lines that could keep you playing for years.

DAUNTLESS

FREE 2 PLAY THE GOLDEN RULES

■ Free 2 Play games have to make their money somewhere, but don't spend if you don't want to or need to. Your parents should be involved in any in-game spending, and you can follow our golden rules.

1 Don't use real money to buy features or cosmetics if you can do it using in-game currency. It might take you a while to earn it, but if the game is fun, who cares?

2 Don't feel that you have to unlock every area, mount, weapon, or costume, even if your favorite influencers keep on pushing it in their Twitch streams or YouTube videos. Enjoy what you have and save your pocket money for things that will improve your experience of the game.

3 Some Free 2 Play games try to hustle you into spending by adding annoying delays into the game play or asking you to collect endless resources that are (shock) available to buy! Don't get suckered in. Take some time out from the game and find something else to play.

4 Season passes are great if you're seriously into a game, but the costs soon add up over a year. Only get them for the game you're most invested in, and watch for games that switch seasons too regularly without adding in new content to make them worth your while.

5 Don't spend any real money on impulse, especially if you don't know exactly what you're getting. Crates that promise exotic weapons and armor might sound exciting, but you might not get what you hoped for—or you might get something you've already had before!

FALL GUYS

FREE 2 PLAY COMPETITIVE AND SPORTS

DISNEY SPEEDSTORM

■ *MultiVersus* has quickly established itself as one of the best multiplayer fighting games out there. It mixes characters from across different Warner Bros. franchises, covering everything from classic cartoons to DC superheroes to the adult fantasy series *Game of Thrones*, and the game play is top notch. If you'd rather party than practice your fighting skills, *Fall Guys* is always good for a laugh! Forcing your jelly bean heroes through deadly obstacle courses never gets tired, and the levels and special events just keep on getting better!

■ *Rocket League* is another legendary effort—its cars-meets-soccer game play hits just the right balance between awesome scoring skills and total chaos. And while it's been long delayed, we reckon *Disney Speedstorm* was held back for all the right reasons, making sure it lives up to its potential as a fantastic, character-focused kart racing game!

NEED FOR SPEED UNBOUND

TAKING RACING BACK TO THE STREETS

Life is tough for racers on the streets of Lakeshore City. The mayor hates your guts, the police are cracking down, and you need to grind for every dollar you can get. If you don't, you won't have the cash to enter the big championship, The Grand, or buy the cars and upgrades that you'll need to win it. This isn't the kind of game that doles out supercars like cookies. If you want to finish first and drive the city's sweetest rides, you're going to have to work!

That's my superstar, always hustling! I'll catch you later tonight. Peace.

QUICK TIPS

UPGRADE YOUR RIDE
■ You won't get anywhere near first place with the basic cars—you need to buy upgrades in the garage. Focus on those that drive your top speed up and reduce your 0 to 60 acceleration times, and you might start to pick up wins.

PAY TO PLAY
■ You won't earn much money if you stick to races without any buy-in cost all the time. Once a day, put your money where your mouth is on a race you think you have a chance of winning. You'll have more chance of a big payout.

QUICK REPAIRS
■ Smashed up your ride while racing? Do the cops keep ramming you off the road? Keep an eye out for the nearest gas station. Simply driving through will get your car repaired—and give you a chance to get to a safe house in one piece!

LIFE, ONE MILE AT A TIME

■ Want to make it big as a racer in Lakeshore? You need to make the most of your time. Each week ends with a qualifying event for The Grand, and you have two sessions every day where you can join a race, run side missions, and earn some serious cash.

HIT THE GAS
■ There are always two or more Meetings where you can pick a race to join. Whether it's a point-to-point sprint or a tense street circuit race, you'll need a great car and all your skills to win.

FRIENDS AND RIVALS
■ Throughout the story, you'll keep coming across the city's elite street racers. Some might become friends if you do them a favor, or you can earn extra cash by making side bets with your rivals.

FAST FACT

Need for Speed is one of the longest-running franchises in gaming. It first appeared nearly thirty years ago in 1994, and this is the twenty-fifth *Need for Speed* in the main series.

RISK OR REWARD
■ Delivering cars will earn you extra money, and you can get more by doing it fast without causing any serious damage. Just watch out: some might be stolen. The cops will be right on your tail!

STYLE IT OUT
■ It's not enough to win—you have to look good while you do it. That means driving the coolest cars and customizing them, and unlocking new graffiti effects that express your awesome drifts and boosts.

MAKE YOUR GETAWAY

■ The more races you win, or the more damage you do escaping the police, the more heat you'll attract and the more cops you're going to have to escape. What's the best way to get away?

DON'T GET SPOTTED

■ The police cars won't chase you if they don't spot you. Use the mini-map to track their movements, and try to avoid driving past them or getting in their sight line. Sometimes you need to go slow, but sometimes you need to speed up!

HOT PURSUIT!

■ Sometimes you can outrun the police; at other times you have to outdrive them. Take sharp corners at the last minute or try heading off-road. They can't always follow.

PLAY IT SAFE

■ When you've escaped, try to make it to Rydell's Garage or the nearest safe house. You can only enter when you're not being chased.

CHECKPOINTS, RAMPS, AND BILLBOARDS

■ Even when you're not racing, you could still be doing something useful. Look for the billboards, ramps, and speed checks around the city. Find ways to smash the billboards and make long jumps off the ramps—and just drive through the checkpoints as fast as you can!

TAKEOVER TIPS

■ Takeover events can be brilliant fun—once you've worked out how they work!

TAKEOVER

BUILD YOUR BONUS

■ The trick is to keep building the bonus multiplier, and never let it drop back to X1. Smashing through barrels and barriers, drifting, sliding, and boosting will all increase your score and keep your bonus growing.

1 / Obi		**103,689**
2 / Dal-Rae		**86,402**
3 / Chilton		**70,130**
4 / Tobias360		

Ⓐ CONTINUE

SCORES OVER SPEED

■ Your Takeover task isn't winning the race but scoring as many points as you can to hit the top of the scoreboard. Driving fast around the circuit gets you nowhere!

SCORES TO BEAT
YOU'RE UP NEXT

DON'T LOSE IT!

■ Driving into walls or flipping the car will lose your bonus, but you can also lose it if you don't keep scoring. If your bonus starts flashing, watch out! Drift or boost to keep hold of that multiplier.

MIX THINGS UP

■ Try to take different routes around the course for each of the three laps. You'll find new barrels and barriers to smash and new opportunities to jump, drift, and boost. Sweet!

LIKE THIS? TRY THIS:

DIRT 5

■ Looking for some dirty, off-road racing? *DIRT 5* will give it to you. You get a great car selection and a lot of different racing styles to try, and it takes place all around the world!

Forza Motorsport

Forget the rest. With Forza Motorsport, racing gets real!

■ After seven hit games and starting up the *Forza Horizon* series, *Forza Motorsport* has had the reboot treatment. The team at Turn 10 Studios promised *Forza* fans a huge generational leap from *Forza Motorsport 7*—and that's what it has delivered, with even more realistic physics, authentic handling, and stunning ray-traced visuals. While it goes easier on new drivers than some hardcore racing simulators, you won't find many driving games that feel this believable—or that have the jaw-dropping graphics to match.

Grab the wheel

■ Turn 10 has pushed *Forza Motorsport*'s physics engine way past previous games to give you the most convincing driving feel. Where it used to simulate a single point of contact between the tire and the track, it now simulates two—and 360 times per second, too! Handling doesn't get much more realistic than this.

FAST FACT

The Maple Valley Raceway track was introduced in the very first *Forza* and has appeared in every game except *Forza 5* and *Forza 6*. It's been transformed with autumn trees and a rushing river on the trackside, making it even more beautiful to drive!

Feel the track

■ The new *Forza* goes the extra mile for realism. It simulates the compounds used in the tire, the wear and tear on the track, and even the temperature of the track and any water on the surface. You can almost feel the track through your wheel or controller.

24 hours

■ *Forza*'s new dynamic lighting system means you can drive races day or night, with some of the most realistic headlight effects you've ever seen in a racing game. Meanwhile, weather effects give you puddles, mud, and spray to deal with. Are you up to the challenge?

Dirt and damage

■ You know how some racing games only play at car damage? On its toughest settings, *Forza* isn't messing around. Drive badly and start trading paint with rival racers, and your car will pick up dents and scratches or the chassis will crumple—or worse! Good luck getting record times with that!

Check the reflections

■ Ray-traced reflections, which simulate how light bounces off different materials, mean the cars' bodywork gleams in a way that makes the world's most exciting sports cars look totally awesome. And Turn 10 has gone to incredible amounts of detail, modeling everything from the smallest rivets to almost every part of the mighty engines.

FREEDOM PLANET 2

UNBELIEVABLE RETRO ACTION MEETS CLASSIC SONIC VIBES

2 097   04

```
A    Dragon Cyclone
X    Rising Slash
B    D
Y    G
```

Looking for a trip back to a world of old-school platform action, where scrappy animal mascots were everywhere and Sonic was their undisputed king? With *Freedom Planet 2*, you've got it. In fact, you get even more, with four playable heroes, an epic story, some blasting, cool character progression, and breakneck speeds. It's the action-packed, retro platformer you've been waiting for.

The destruction of the Kingdom Stone in the first *Freedom Planet* has freed Merga the water dragon from her centuries-old prison. Now, Merga's back and causing chaos in the realm of Avalice, attempting to revive an ancient weapon. Can the girls of Team Lilac, plus their old rival, Neera Li, put a stop to Merga's plans?

QUICK TIPS

0 136   12'39"60

HARNESS YOUR POWERS
■ Each hero has their own unique attacks, so don't just spam the basic attack button. Lilac's Dragon Boost or Milla's Phantom Cube blast can wear down tougher enemies and bosses faster.

KEEP MOVING
■ You don't have to blast every bad guy. Sometimes combat only slows you down, while many enemies can be dodged or just avoided. Don't sweat it if you don't need to.

STUCK?
■ If you find your way blocked, backtrack and explore. There may be another route through that you haven't spotted, or a switch that will open up your way.

PLANET OF ADVENTURE

■ *Freedom Planet 2* is one big adventure—and you're free to play it your way. You can dig deep into the combat, go for the speed-run records, or spend your time exploring, with a choice of Classic and Adventure modes to let you focus on the action or get the most out of the story.

MEET TEAM LILAC

■ Each of our four heroes has their own cool play style. Lilac's built for speed, while Milla is ready to explore. Carol is a fierce close-combat brawler, and Neera has some amazing power moves.

LILAC THE DRAGON

THE BIGGER THEY ARE . . .

■ It wouldn't be a great retro platformer without massive, screen-filling bosses. These guys take some work to bring down, but look for the weak spots and keep dodging or blocking their attacks.

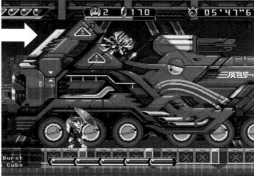

SONIC SPEEDS

■ Like the stages in a classic *Sonic* game, *Freedom Planet*'s levels are built for speed. Ramps, chutes, loops, and springs keep you moving fast, and you can even grind the rails on a roller coaster!

IT'S ALL ABOUT MOMENTUM

■ Some of these stages get pretty challenging, but hold your nerve and keep pushing forward. Every level has different routes to explore, where you can head high or low—or smash straight through!

FAST FACT

Freedom Planet hero Sash Lilac began life as a hedgehog in a fan-made *Sonic* tribute game. She was transformed into a water dragon for *Freedom Planet*, but you can still see the hedgehog heritage in her incredible speed and special moves.

LIKE THIS? TRY THIS:

SONIC MANIA

■ *Sonic Mania* recaptures the magic of the early *Sonic* games, complete with awesome pixel art and an unbeatable set of stages. Some people think it's the greatest *Sonic* ever!

MASTER PLATFORM GAMES

Struggling with Sonic? Broken by the Bandicoot? Read our crash course in playing platform games.

Platform games can be challenging, especially if you're new to the adventures of Mario, Sonic, and their mates. Getting better takes time and practice, but it also helps to have an understanding of how the platform game works. That's where we can help. With the aid of classic platform games and heroes, including Rayman, Crash Bandicoot, Sonic, and Mario, we're going to give you the fundamentals plus tips and tricks to help you finish every level.

BEYOND THE BASICS

■ We're going to assume that you know how to run and jump, and that you've got the basic spin or punch moves down if your game features that kind of thing. However, some moves aren't quite so obvious.

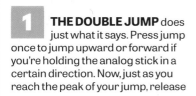

1 **THE DOUBLE JUMP** does just what it says. Press jump once to jump upward or forward if you're holding the analog stick in a certain direction. Now, just as you reach the peak of your jump, release and press jump again to extend it. You'll get farther or higher! Some games replace the standard double jump with a handy hover or glide. This is also great for crossing longer gaps or making a safe landing if you're falling.

FAST
FACT

3 THE DOWNWARD SMASH
(otherwise known as the Butt Stomp) is great for crushing or stunning tougher enemies, bashing in wooden pegs or buttons, or smashing through weak bits of the floor. Jump, then as you're falling, press the crawl or stomp button. Your hero will take on extra weight and drop through anything (or anyone) as they drop.

4 SWINGING
should be the easy way to get across a gap, but you have to get the timing right. Jump onto the rope, then press jump again, just before you reach the highest point of the swing. This should give your jump maximum height and length. If you can climb up and down the rope, stick near the bottom to get the biggest swing and the most distance.

2 WALL JUMPS are useful when you have a narrow area with walls on both sides. Jump toward one wall, then when you make contact, press jump to rebound off it toward the wall on the other side. When you reach that wall, jump again. You can usually chain several jumps together. In some games, you may also need to hold left or right with each jump.

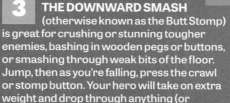

HAZARDS AND OBSTACLES

■ Levels are designed to make things tricky for your hero, with obstacles and perils that can stop you reaching the end—or just result in your destruction! You can get past them. It just takes practice.

1 **DISAPPEARING PLATFORMS** are a nightmare for platform game heroes, but they usually don't disappear or crumble straightaway. Learn what they look like, then try to cross them as quickly as possible. If there are several in a row, try to time it so that you can land, run, and jump from each one in a smooth chain of moves. It might take a few tries to get right, but it will get you to the other side!

2 **FROM MARIO'S FALLING THWOMPS** to swinging blades, crushing ceilings, and jets of fire, platform games are chock-full of dangerous objects doing their best to squash, slice, or scorch you. However, these things always work to a pattern. Watch when they drop, flame, or swing into the danger zone, then try to work out how long you've got while they're resetting or moving out of the way. Now time your move so that you pass them just after they're dangerous, giving you maximum time to run or jump past and reach safety.

3 **MOVING PLATFORMS** can be a challenge, but—again—it's all about the timing. Be patient and wait until you can walk or jump easily from one platform to another to make your move. If the platform moves in a way that might tip you off, things get a bit more challenging. Move fast and try to jump onto a part of the surface that will stay horizontal. Otherwise, you're in for a nasty drop!

4 **BAD GUYS!** Who needs them? If they're not planning to whack you or blast you, they're getting in the way so that you'll touch them and take some damage as you try to get from A to B. Sometimes there's nothing you can do except avoid them, but if your character has a punch, jump, or dash attack, now is the time to use it. Hit them before they hit you, or watch for an opening after they try to attack and give 'em a thumping!

MOVES LIKE MARIO

■ Every platform hero has their share of slick moves, but Mario has a whole bunch of moves that new players might not be aware of. In many games he has a spin jump, called in if you rotate the movement stick before jumping. He also has a backward or sideways jump, where you stand facing one direction, then press jump while flicking the stick in the opposite direction, or sideways left or right. These jumps will give you maximum height.

■ Mario's most legendary move is the triple jump. Tap the jump button to make the first jump, then again as Mario lands, and he'll jump longer and farther with the second jump. Now jump again as he lands the second jump, and he'll pull off one final epic leap!

GENERAL STRATEGIES

GO WITH THE FLOW
■ Some games or levels are all about speed, and you'll actually find them harder if you try to take them slow. Instead, be bold, keep moving forward, and make the most of all those springs, loops, and chutes. Grab rings, coins, and power-ups. They'll give you a second chance if you take damage.

WATCH FOR SNEAKY TRAPS
■ Platform game designers have a nasty habit of putting a hazard right at the end of a fast-moving section. Watch out for this and prepare to jump or dodge. You're done with falling for their tricks!

FOLLOW THE COLLECTIBLES
■ Rings, coins, and other collectibles help make the platform gaming world go round, but designers also use them to lead you toward goals or secret power-ups and areas. If a trail of coins or rings seems to be going out of your way, try following it. You never know what you will find.

NOTHING'S OUT OF REACH
■ If a collectible or power-up is out of reach, then there's always a way to reach it. You might have to take another route and smash through a wall or drop down through the floor, or you might be able to ride an airflow upward, then double jump across to grab that hovering star.

GET A BOOST
■ If you run out of puff trying to make it up a slope or across a gap, look for anything that can give your hero a speed boost. Boost rings, launchers, speed pads, and cannons are all great for acceleration—usefully, the designers will often place one nearby.

USE FOES TO GET PLACES
■ Sometimes enemies are obstacles, but at other times you can use them to get to where you need to go. In the *Sonic* games, for instance, Sonic's spin attack move will often target enemies you'd never reach by jumping, and you can chain several attacks together to cross huge stretches of a level.

PAY ATTENTION
■ Platform games are full of secrets. Keep looking for ways you can use the tools and powers in the game to smash down a wall, burst through a floor, or take on a different route. For instance, explosives will cause you damage, but they might also take out a wall that's hiding something cool. Don't just blast through every level. Try to work out what else you could be missing!

DISNEY ILLUSION ISLAND

Join Mickey, Minnie, Donald, and Goofy in their biggest adventure yet

Love the old-school Disney cartoon antics of *The Wonderful World of Mickey Mouse*? *Disney Illusion Island* brings them to life in one incredible platform game. And like *Super Mario Bros. U* or *Rayman Legends*, it's a game that's been designed to be enjoyed with friends. So, what are you waiting for? Find some friends to join the fun as Minnie, Donald, and Goofy, and test your wits and your platforming skills!

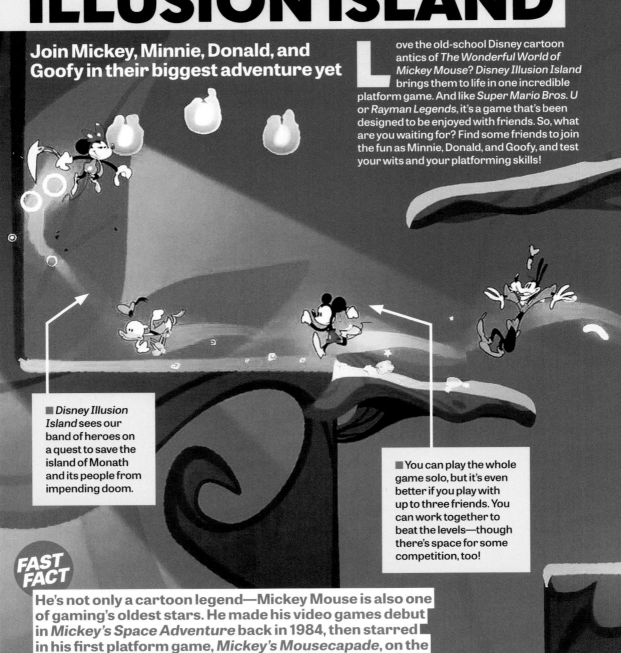

■ *Disney Illusion Island* sees our band of heroes on a quest to save the island of Monath and its people from impending doom.

■ You can play the whole game solo, but it's even better if you play with up to three friends. You can work together to beat the levels—though there's space for some competition, too!

FAST FACT

He's not only a cartoon legend—Mickey Mouse is also one of gaming's oldest stars. He made his video games debut in *Mickey's Space Adventure* back in 1984, then starred in his first platform game, *Mickey's Mousecapade*, on the original Nintendo Entertainment System in 1998!

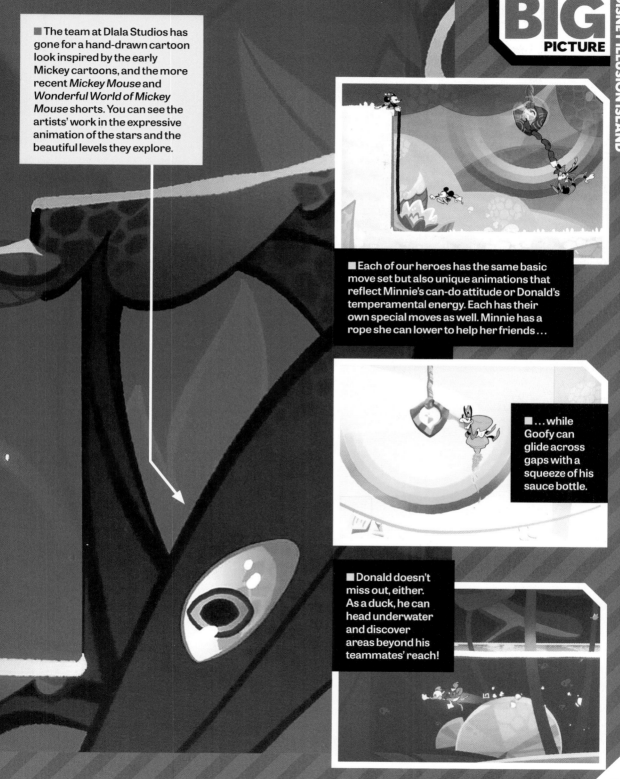

■ The team at Dlala Studios has gone for a hand-drawn cartoon look inspired by the early Mickey cartoons, and the more recent *Mickey Mouse* and *Wonderful World of Mickey Mouse* shorts. You can see the artists' work in the expressive animation of the stars and the beautiful levels they explore.

■ Each of our heroes has the same basic move set but also unique animations that reflect Minnie's can-do attitude or Donald's temperamental energy. Each has their own special moves as well. Minnie has a rope she can lower to help her friends ...

■ ... while Goofy can glide across gaps with a squeeze of his sauce bottle.

■ Donald doesn't miss out, either. As a duck, he can head underwater and discover areas beyond his teammates' reach!

SONIC FRONTIERS

THE START OF A SONIC BOOM?

It's a long time since Sonic has been on an epic 3D adventure, but *Sonic Frontiers* is the comeback game that fans have been waiting for. It takes our hedgehog hero to the Starfall Islands—an area of ancient ruins and unearthly mystery—where strange forces separate Sonic from his friends. Can he find his buddies, collect the Chaos Emeralds, and defeat a dark entity that threatens two worlds? If you know anything about Sonic, then you're going to bet on the blue blur.

QUICK TIPS

TAKE A THRILL RIDE
■ The Starfall Islands are packed with sneaky springs, floating grind rails, speed pads, and boost rings that can be used to launch Sonic onto hidden routes and challenge trails. If you see one, try it. You never know where you'll end up or what you'll find there.

PRACTICE MAKES PERFECT
■ Each Cyber Space mission has at least three challenges beyond just reaching the end goal. To collect enough Vault Keys you'll need to complete at least one of these, so keep going back to get the rings or the red star coins, even if you're struggling to post a record time.

USE THE SEEDS
■ Defeat enemies and complete challenges and you'll collect the Red and Blue Seeds. Take these to Hermit Koco and he'll upgrade Sonic's offensive and defensive powers. Sweet!

NEW FRONTIERS OF ADVENTURE

■ The Starfall Islands aren't like anywhere that Sonic has been before. They're a whole lot bigger, and the spiky speedster has much more freedom to explore. With portals to open, vaults to unlock, and gigantic Guardians to battle, this hedgehog has his work cut out!

ISLAND LIFE
■ At first you'll only have small areas of the islands to explore, but start beating challenges and opening portals and the game's massive world opens up.

FAST FACT

Sonic originally started out as a rabbit when his artist, Naoto Ohshima, worked on the original game. At one point he almost became an armadillo, before the team settled on the spiky superstar we know today.

ENTER CYBER SPACE
■ As well as exploring the open world, Sonic has to complete Cyber Space missions. These play out like classic Sonic 2D and 3D levels, so you'll need all your high-speed skills to survive.

MEET THE LOCALS
■ Some of the locals just aren't friendly. As well as evil robot menaces and electrifying enemies, you'll meet screen-filling Guardians and the even bigger Titans.

ENJOY THE VIEW
■ Unlock the vaults and rescue Sonic's besties and you'll open up new areas to explore. Prepare to race along vertical walls, loop the loop, and fly through the air.

EMERALD HUNTER

01:28:05

■ *Sonic Frontiers* gives you freedom to explore, but it's tough at first working out where to go and what to do. Your main mission on each island is to collect six Chaos Emeralds, but getting them won't be easy. Some are locked away in vaults, which need a set of keys to open. Others can only be collected by completing tasks for Sonic's friends—and you've got to restore their memories first!

BEAT THE LEVELS
■ The best way to get Vault Keys is to win them in the Cyber Space levels. Whether they revive classic 2D Sonic levels or play out in full 3D, you need to collect all the rings and red coins you can and hit the finish as fast as you can.

FIGHT THE GUARDIANS
■ Cyber Space levels are accessed through the portals, but to unlock them you'll need Portal Gears. You can win these by defeating enemies, but the most certain way to get them is to defeat the island's deadly Guardians. Each of these hulking horrors is a mini boss battle in its own right!

GONE FISHIN'

MISSING MEMORIES
■ Sonic's friends have Chaos Emeralds, but you need to find them, restore their memories, and complete their final tasks. The missing memories can be found by completing challenges or by reaching the highest and most distant areas of the map. Follow every trail to track them down.

■ Finding life on the Starfall Islands hectic? Take some time out to go fishing with your old pal Big the Cat. While you catch your share of minnows and whoppers, you can also hook a treasure chest with a gold ticket that you can swap for a Portal Gear or key! Fish can be traded for tokens that you can spend on memories, seeds, and other goodies.

SUPER SONIC SHOWDOWN

■ Collect all the Chaos Emeralds on an island and it's time to take on its Titan boss. These guys are seriously huge, but don't worry. With the power of the Chaos Emeralds, Sonic can transform into Super Sonic and defeat them!

■ It still won't be easy, though. Each of these boss battles is an epic, with the Titans getting tougher as you fight them. Our tips? Master Sonic's combat moves before you go into battle—his sidestep and parry moves are particularly important—and collect all the rings you can before you make each attempt. These big guys will bash the rings from Sonic like there's no tomorrow, so it helps to have a lot to play with.

LIKE THIS? **TRY THIS:**

CRASH BANDICOOT 4: IT'S ABOUT TIME
■ Crash Bandicoot's comeback adventure is one of the smartest and most inventive 3D platform games of the last ten years, and it looks stunning on the latest consoles, with some truly awesome levels to push through. Not played it? It's about time that you did!

GAMES GO TO *the* MOVIES

Is Hollywood finally making good movies of the world's greatest games?

For decades it seemed impossible to turn video games into good movies. From early fails like the 1993 *Super Mario Bros.* and 1994 *Street Fighter* movies to big budget flops like *Prince of Persia: The Sands of Time* (2010), Hollywood seemed unable to take characters and stories from the games we loved and make them something that anyone should watch.

In the past few years, that's changed. After a shocking early trailer, 2020's *Sonic the Hedgehog* turned out to be pretty good, and 2019's *Pokémon Detective Pikachu* managed to be a funny, smart, and believable take on a Pokémon world. Meanwhile, 2023's *Super Mario Bros.* movie packs in nearly everything fans love about Mario and his magical Mushroom Kingdom world. Are movies based on games getting better, or what?

BRINGING GAMES TO LIFE

■ Some of this comes down to the technology. When making the 1993 *Super Mario Bros.*, the filmmakers couldn't rely on computer-generated graphics. Instead, they had to work with elaborate costumes, makeup, puppets, and practical effects that could be pulled off in front of the camera. Bowser—or King Koopa, as he was called at the time—is played by the actor Dennis Hopper with his hair gelled into ridges, wearing a sharp business suit. Yoshi the dinosaur is a puppet, and even the Goombas are guys in overcoats with shrunken dinosaur heads!

He definitely looks like Pikachu to us

This isn't the Yoshi we know and love!

■ Contrast that with today's game movies. The 2023 *Super Mario Bros.* movie is all CGI, meaning you get the Bowser we know and love to hate, the Mushroom Kingdom in all its glory, plus Mario's friends and foes in their familiar forms. Even live-action movies, like the *Sonic* movies and *Pokémon Detective Pikachu*, have the effects and budgets to re-create scenes and characters from the game. When you see Sonic take on the Death Egg Robot in *Sonic the Hedgehog 2*,

you're watching a big moment from the game brought to life.

■ Similarly, *Pokémon Detective Pikachu* stuffed its scenes full of Pokémon doing what we expect Pokémon to do. The underground fight club sequence alone has over thirty different species visible, with over sixty digital Pokémon mixing in with the live-action crowd. And when you see Magikarp or Psyduck, you're seeing the characters you know from the game.

LEARNING ABOUT GAMES

■ It also helps that the people making these movies work more closely with the people who make the original games, and that they now have years of detailed concept art and 3D models to work with. When director Rob Letterman worked on Pikachu's character for *Pokémon Detective Pikachu*, he worked directly with Ken Sugimori, the character's original designer, who oversaw all the movie's concept art. Meanwhile, the team at the visual effects

workshop, Framestore, spent months researching the characters thoroughly, checking out the games and cartoons to make sure each monster had the right look and signature moves. The idea wasn't to reinvent the characters, but give them a form that could work in a live-action world.

■ What's more, the filmmakers of today have grown up playing games. When they took on the challenge of transforming

Super Mario Bros. into the 1993 movie, directors Rocky Morton and Annabel Jankel took more inspiration from Tim Burton's 1989 film of *Batman* and came up with a darker science fiction concept based on an alternate dimension where dinosaurs had evolved. They hoped for a family-friendly movie that would also be a hit with adults. The result? A weird cyberpunk Mario movie that doesn't look or feel like a Mario game.

■ Today's writers, artists, and directors know fans want a good story, but one that doesn't ditch the characters and worlds of the games. Jeff Fowler, the director of *Sonic the Hedgehog* and its sequel, felt that the most important thing was to make Sonic a character that the audience could root for—an outsider looking for friends and a family. And when there was bad feedback over the infamous "ugly Sonic" of the trailers, Fowler and his team went back to work to get the hedgehog right. The second film added in more characters—like Tails and Knuckles—that the fans wanted to see, along with scenes that played on iconic moments from the games. *Sonic 2* gives Sonic the movie he deserves.

■ Similarly, Rob Letterman worked to make sure that *Pokémon*

Detective Pikachu connected to the overall *Pokémon* universe, with monsters, easter eggs, and Mewtwo plotlines that fans could recognize from the cartoon series and games. Nobody wants to see a film that just re-creates levels from a game; today's audiences are much more aware of the games and what happens in them, and they want to see the stuff they know. You only have to see the way the 2023 *Super Mario Bros.* packs in its glass tubes, karts, and Tanooki costumes to see that the filmmakers get this.

■ Even the actors are fans these days. Jack Black told a New York Comic Con Q&A in 2022 that playing Bowser in the *Super Mario Bros.* movie was "a lot of pressure, because Bowser is known and loved by millions around the world for years. He's one of the greatest video game villains of all time." Black revealed that one of his earliest video game memories was playing the *Donkey Kong* arcade

The *Sonic* movies get Sonic's appeal

game at the mini-mart in Culver City where he grew up, and that he's watched the series evolve. Being a fan meant Black could bring out Bowser's more sensitive side, along with his rage and "heavy-metal, rock-star style."

■ We're still going to get our share of bad video game movies, but at least we can hope that some will turn out good—or even great. And it's all because Hollywood is learning to understand video games and the video game audience—and even treat both with a little respect!

Jack Black gave Bowser rock-star style

THE BEST

2022

SONIC THE HEDGEHOG 2

■ The first *Sonic* movie did a great job of introducing the blue blur to a new generation of fans. The second went further, giving Jim Carrey's Robotnik his original iconic look, and re-creating more scenes and stars from the classic Sega games.

2022

UNCHARTED

■ The Tom Holland movie of the awesome Naughty Dog action-adventure series doesn't try to re-create the story lines of the games, instead working as a kind of prequel that captures their spirit and daredevil action. It's not perfect, but it's a great start.

2019

POKÉMON DETECTIVE PIKACHU

■ *Pokémon Detective Pikachu* has it all: a star turn from Ryan Reynolds as the world's cutest detective, a script that's laugh-out-loud funny, and a supporting cast of fan-favorite Pokémon that don't look weird in a live-action film.

2016

RATCHET AND CLANK

■ The movie was partly written by one of the writers of the *Ratchet and Clank Future* trilogy of games, while the games' makers, Insomniac, helped out with the screenplay and 3D character design. It feels like a natural evolution of the series, featuring all of its most-loved stars.

THE WORST

SUPER MARIO BROS.

■ The first *Super Mario Bros.* movie is one of cinema's most legendary flops. Plagued by script rewrites during production and arguments on the set, it ditched the familiar Mario settings and most of the characters for a gritty sci-fi take.

1993

1994

STREET FIGHTER

■ Hollywood took Capcom's blockbuster fighting game and turned it into a vehicle for nineties action star Jean-Claude Van Damme. It's not all bad, with a scene-stealing performance from Raul Julia as M. Bison, but the fight scenes are clumsy and the Guile-heavy plot woefully bad.

MARIO + RABBIDS: GAMING'S WEIRDEST CROSSOVER RETURNS!
SPARKS OF HOPE

Who knew that the *Mario + Rabbids* combo could be so brilliant? And who would have bet on an even better second game? *Sparks of Hope* has Mario, Luigi, and Princess Peach teaming up once again with their Raving Rabbid friends. This time they're battling Cursa—an evil entity spreading Darkness across the galaxy by absorbing all the energy from the shining hybrid Rabbid/Lumas known as Sparks.

Exploring different planets and fighting Cursa's minions, our heroes have their work cut out. But with a squad of new Rabbid warriors, not to mention the mighty Bowser, there's no way that these guys are going to lose!

QUICK TIPS

SPLASH THE CASH
■ Every planet has a handful of shops where you can buy Super Mushrooms, POW Blocks, reset timers, and the like. Buy a selection before a tough battle. It will help your team survive.

FOCUS ON THE OBJECTIVE
■ Not every battle is won by defeating all your enemies. In missions where you have to reach a certain point or beat a certain foe, move fast and concentrate on the goal.

FIND SOME COVER
■ If possible, end each turn behind cover, so that your enemies don't get an easy shot. Even a hero can be brought down by gunfire if they're left out in the open.

A BAND OF HEROES

■ Cursa and its crew of monsters are after the power of the Sparks. Only Mario, his friends, and those wacky Rabbids stand in their way!

FISTS OF FURY
■ Rabbid Mario is one mighty brawler, with moves designed to punish any enemy that gets too close. This Rabbid is fast and fierce in combat, but weak on defense from ranged attacks.

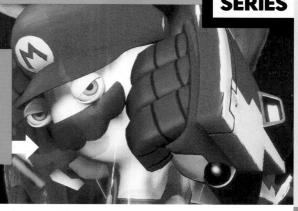

CUTTING EDGE
■ With a mighty sword and punky style, Edge is like no Rabbid that we've seen before. Her flying blade puts fear into foes in cover, while her Stormblade technique teaches bullies a lesson.

BRIGHT SPARKS
■ The Sparks aren't just there to be rescued. Beat their captors in battle and they'll join your team, adding new attacks and protective perks to any hero you assign them to.

ULTIMATE BAD BOY
■ What's Bowser doing, fighting on the side of good? Who cares! He's as hard as nails, with a Bowzooka that deals out damage across a wide area and the ability to summon mechanical minions.

FAST FACT

The lovable Rabbids were originally meant to be the bad guys in a *Rayman* platform game. Instead, that game was canceled and they became the stars of their own bonkers party games!

LIKE THIS? TRY THIS:

TRIANGLE STRATEGY
■ This fantastic RPG from the makers of *Octopath Traveler* and *Final Fantasy* is another great mix of battle strategy and adventure. The choices you make can transform the whole story!

MARIO + RABBIDS: SPARKS OF HOPE

All the skills and strategies you need to win

Mario + Rabbids: Sparks of Hope isn't going to test your reflexes, but it is going to give your brains a workout. To win these battles, you'll need to know your heroes' strengths and weaknesses and work out strategies to beat your foes. You'll also need to use the scenery to your advantage and learn when and where to use your mightiest attacks. Struggling to grab those victories? These tips should help.

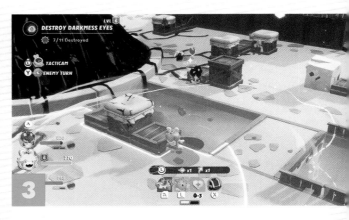

Sniper with a death stare

■ Luigi might be a notorious coward, but he's a great help on the battlefield. Get him to a high spot and use him to take out distant enemies, and make the most of his Steely Stare ability. Activate it, and the first enemy that moves is going to find out the hard way about Luigi's eagle eye.

Dash and jump

■ It's easy to underestimate the Dash and Team Jump moves. Team Jump can get your heroes into high positions for sniping or extend their movement to get them closer, faster, to their goal. The Dash is basically a free close-combat attack, and essential for tackling Bob-ombs and Goombas.

Make the most of Rabbid Peach

■ Rabbid Peach's healing capabilities can be a lifesaver, giving any hero in range a health boost when they need it most. But that's not the end of her uses. Her Triple-Troll is one of the few weapons that can hit enemies out of line of sight and in cover.

Match your team to the objectives

■ Check out the objectives and the position of enemies on the map before you pick your team for battle. Sometimes it helps to have a hero like Edge or Rabbid Mario who's good in a close-up scrap, while at other times you'll wish you had a healer or a hero with protective skills.

4

Y FAST FORWARD

5

Accept the challenge

■ You don't need to fight every battle in the game, and sometimes you can dodge an enemy, or even run away! All the same, completing the secondary missions can be worth it, as you'll earn experience, Star Bits, and coins, all of which will come in handy when the big fights come.

6

Leave your attack until last

■ The main attack move is the last thing your hero can do in any turn, so don't select it until you've moved, used any techniques or Spark abilities, and—if you're smart—gotten behind some cover. Sometimes it's worth staying out in the open to destroy a weak enemy, but be careful. Too much courage can get your heroes killed!

20 % CHANCE   254 DMG

SHARPSHOOTER 174 - 196 DMG
Fires one projectile. The farther the target, the more damage it deals.

Ⓐ   Ⓑ

7

HEROES   TEAM   SPARKS   ITEMS

PYROSTAR
LVL 3   0/200
NEXT LEVEL

GIVE A STAR BIT
A Star Bit will give some XP to a Spark.
779
Ⓐ FEED

Bonus for the next level:
BURN ATTACK
+10% WEAPON DMG USAGE
130% 140%

GIVE A STAR POTION
A Star Potion will automatically level up a Spark.
0

BURN PROTECTOR
-5% DMG
-25% -30%

Find more Starpotions with Salesbot 9.99+TX or by completing more Quests!

Ⓑ BACK

Level up your Sparks

■ Learning new skills is obvious, but it's easy to forget about your Sparks. Feed them Star Bits or Star Potions and you'll power up their abilities, making them a whole lot more useful in a scrap.

You'll get plenty of Star Bits in battle, and you can always buy the potions in the store. Focus on the Sparks you use with your regular heroes, but don't be afraid to mix things up and try a new combo!

AVATAR: FRONTIERS OF PANDORA

Explore the living world of the *Avatar* movies

Pandora, the world of *Avatar*, is one of the all-time great sci-fi worlds, and *Avatar: Frontiers of Pandora* does a spectacular job of bringing it to life. As a Na'vi warrior, it's up to you to protect Pandora and its strange and wonderful life-forms from the mineral-greedy forces of the human Resources Development Administration. Watch out—these life-forms can be just as deadly!

■ Your Na'vi hero might be up against armed troops with guns and killer mech suits, but you're far from defenseless. You're a master of the bow and equipped with poisoned and explosive arrows. Fight to protect Pandora!

■ The Western Frontier has its share of deadly beasts, but you can rely on the Na'vis' natural bond with some of its six-limbed animals. Remember the direhorse? It's your mount while you're on the land, enabling you to cross huge areas at speed.

■ When you need to take to the air, it's time to jump on the back of a banshee. The flying creatures of *Avatar* are yours to ride, as long as you can survive the rite of bonding.

■ The flora and fauna of Pandora's jungles is bioluminescent—both plants and animals glow with a natural light. What's more, the plants will react to how you move and behave toward them. Be gentle and stay on your toes if you don't want trouble.

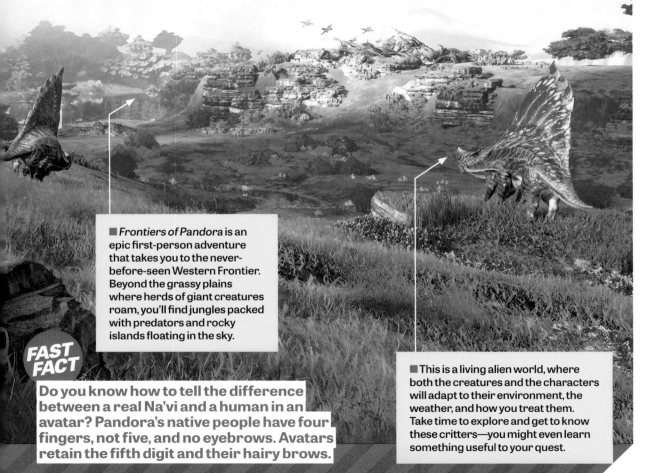

■ *Frontiers of Pandora* is an epic first-person adventure that takes you to the never-before-seen Western Frontier. Beyond the grassy plains where herds of giant creatures roam, you'll find jungles packed with predators and rocky islands floating in the sky.

FAST FACT

Do you know how to tell the difference between a real Na'vi and a human in an avatar? Pandora's native people have four fingers, not five, and no eyebrows. Avatars retain the fifth digit and their hairy brows.

■ This is a living alien world, where both the creatures and the characters will adapt to their environment, the weather, and how you treat them. Take time to explore and get to know these critters—you might even learn something useful to your quest.

MARVEL'S
MIDNIGHT SUNS

SUPERHEROES MEET THE SUPERNATURAL!

When a mad Hydra scientist resurrects Lilith, the mother of demons, who are you going to call to save the world? The Midnight Suns, that's who! A strange crew of demon hunters, vampire slayers, sorceresses, and men possessed by vengeful spirits, they're ready to take on Hydra and an army of twisted supervillains—and send Lilith back where she belongs.

This sizzling-hot superhero strategy game also packs in some more familiar faces—and even allows you to hang out. Have you ever wanted to watch movies with Spider-Man or go fishing with Wolverine? Now's your chance. Make the Avengers your amigos and turn Blade into your bestie, and they'll fight even harder by your side!

QUICK TIPS

KEEP TIME ON YOUR SIDE
■ Some missions have timed objectives that have to be completed in a set number of turns. Focus on these first, or you're sure to miss them.

AVOID A KNOCKOUT
■ Try to use Healing cards and cover to stop heroes from getting knocked out. Sure, you can revive them, but they'll be weak. Why not heal them now?

USE THE ENVIRONMENT
■ A superpowered punch works, but watch out for ways to use the scenery for maximum damage. Can you knock that bad guy back into something explosive or throw that generator at him?

MEET THE MIDNIGHT SUNS

■ You'll recognize the game's Avengers, but what about the less familiar members of the team? Let us introduce you to the Midnight Suns.

THE HUNTER

■ The Hunter is the son or daughter of Lilith herself. The Hunter has been trained by their aunt Sara—the Caretaker—to defeat their malevolent mom and slay any demons who might stop her. You can decide what the Hunter looks like and even customize their clothes!

BLADE

■ Marvel's deadliest vampire hunter is a master of close combat, with attacks that chain together to help him deal with a bunch of enemies at once. He can also make enemies vulnerable with his Bleed ability, and even steal their health with a stake to the heart.

MAGIK

■ Illyana Rasputina started out as the kid sister of the X-Men hero Colossus, but these days she's famous as a mighty sorceress, wielding a magical Soulsword. Many of her powers revolve around portals. Pop one open to another dimension, then shove that enemy through it!

GHOST RIDER

■ Robbie Reyes is the fourth Ghost Rider —a murdered car mechanic resurrected by the first Ghost Rider, Johnny Blaze. Filled with the spirit of vengeance, he transforms into a demonic being with a flaming skull for a head. His fiery chain attacks will drain him of his health, but who cares when they pack such a punch!

FAST FACT

In Marvel's comic books, the Midnight Suns were originally the Midnight Sons, a supergroup of supernatural beings fighting to save the soul of the second Ghost Rider, Danny Ketch. *Midnight Suns*, the game, features two Ghost Riders: Johnny Blaze and Robbie Reyes.

NICO MINORU

■ Originally one of the Runaways, Nico's the goth sorceress with the powerful Staff of One and the bestie of Wanda Maximoff, the Scarlet Witch. As well as strong magical attacks, she has some brilliant support and healing abilities— and she's a lot of fun to hang out with, too!

CARD TRICKS

■ Combat in *Midnight Suns* takes getting used to, as it's a clever mix of turn-based strategy and collectible card games. Struggling to win the fights? We've got a few tips to help.

PICK A CARD
■ You can usually play up to three cards in each turn, and it doesn't matter if they all use the same hero. Some are free to play, but others require heroism points. Playing your free cards first can help you build the points you need.

POSITIONING
■ You can only move one here per turn and their positioning is important. You'll need to be in the right position to knock a bad guy backward with knockback moves, or to use an attack like Captain Marvel's Photon Beam, which can hit multiple enemies if they're standing in a line.

KNOCKBACKS
■ Knockbacks are a great way to get free damage. Hit one guy with a knockback attack and you can shift the knockback target with the mouse or thumbstick, so that he'll smash into the scenery or crash into another foe. If you're lucky, you can grab two KOs for the price of one!

COMBOS
■ Sometimes you can combine hero powers, using one hero's abilities to weaken a tough enemy, then another hero's attack to hit them hard with a lot of damage. Other moves, like Magik's Limbo Portal, are great for setting up an enemy for a follow-up attack.

MEET THE VILLAINS

■ Lilith is the big bad of *Midnight Suns*. Summoned back from the dead by Hydra scientist Doctor Faustus she's now using Hydra for her own evil ends—the resurrection of an ancient god, Chthon.

■ Hydra's soldiers will do anything for the demon they call "Mother." They come with different power levels, weapons, and skills, and are replaced by reinforcements as fast as you can blast them!

■ It's not just Hydra that falls under Lilith's spell. Venom has also been caught by her enchantments, working to destroy Earth's mightiest heroes and have a few snacks along the way!

THE ABBEY

■ When you're not battling Hydra and Lilith's tame supervillains, you'll be relaxing and preparing at your secret base, the Abbey. There's plenty to do while you're off duty—and it will all make your Midnight Suns a more effective super team.

UPGRADE IN THE FORGE

■ Powered by a trapped fire demon, this furnace fuels Doctor Strange and Iron Man's crafting and research. It's here that you can unlock new cars and upgrades, turning artifacts and gamma coils into more powerful gear.

STRATEGIZE IN THE WAR ROOM

■ This is where your hero, the Hunter, and the Caretaker manage their campaign. You can choose missions from the Mirror Table, or send heroes on intel-collecting missions from the C.E.N.T.R.A.L. workstation.

TRAIN IN THE YARD

■ This space doubles as a training arena and a hospital for injured superheroes. Once a day, the Hunter can spar with another superhero, adding useful friendship points, combat bonuses, stat upgrades, and extra XP.

LIKE THIS? TRY THIS:

MARVEL SNAP

■ Love Marvel superheroes? Love the card-based strategy of Midnight Suns? Then why aren't you playing Marvel Snap already? It's a simpler, fast-paced game without a story, but it's brilliant fun.

HANG OUT IN THE COMMON ROOM

■ The Abbey's lounge is a key spot for hangouts, where you can spend time with your favorite heroes to boost your friendships and alter how dark or light the Hunter's powers become. It's a great way to get to know your fellow supes or turn a tricky relationship around.

EXPLORE THE GROUNDS

■ You'll get time to wander outside the Abbey, and there are plenty of secrets to discover. As the game goes on, you'll find new ways to train and upgrade your abilities, and there's a whole side quest around sealed gates for you to discover.

95

The Worlds of SpongeBob SquarePants:
The Cosmic Shake

SpongeBob is lost in a multiverse of madness!

■ Winning the *Battle for Bikini Bottom* was just the start of SpongeBob's gaming career. Since then we've seen him and his friends tearing up the track in *Nickelodeon Kart Racers* and going toe to toe in *Nickelodeon All-Star Brawl*. Now he's back in a new adventure, *SpongeBob SquarePants: The Cosmic Shake*.

■ This time, an encounter with a mysterious fortune teller leaves our hero in possession of wish-granting mermaid's tears. Can he be trusted with this power? Of course not! Before you know it, he's wrecked the very fabric of time and space, leaving SpongeBob and a balloon-ified Patrick on a quest through different dimensions and different eras to save the universe from disaster!

Jurassic jerk
■ SpongeBob's heading back to the dawn of time to embrace his inner caveman. Can he survive a savage world full of savage beasts, or is Bikini Bottom (and the universe) doomed? Watch out for a red-hot, lava-spurting boss confrontation!

Ride 'em, cowboy

■ This Wild West world features canyons and soaring sandstone pillars, giving SpongeBob some perilous platforms to navigate. And don't be surprised if, with trains and seahorses, there's a thrilling chase sequence ahead.

Jeepers creepers!

■ SpongeBob needs his Halloween finest to fit into this ghostly domain. It's a world full of spooky scenery and scary characters, with a few shocking twists along the way and a truly terrifying boss.

Kit yourself out

■ Each new world has new costumes for SpongeBob to try on, bringing him new capabilities that can help him on his journey. Will this slick outfit give him the combat skills of a martial arts master? If it doesn't, don't enter the dojo!

FAST FACT

SpongeBob SquarePants: The Cosmic Shake **comes from Purple Lamp Studios, the same team that brought us** *Battle for Bikini Bottom: Rehydrated.* **The remake was so successful that the studio was signed up to make a brand-new game!**

Always the joker

■ What costume would suit SpongeBob better in this medieval era than a jester's motley suit and cap? Sadly, the beasts and bosses in this magical dimension aren't fans of SpongeBob's slapstick humor.

MADDEN NFL 23

WORTHY OF THE MADDEN NAME

The legendary coach is no longer with us, but John Madden's legacy goes on in EA's awesome football game. *NFL 23* brings some major improvements to game play, new tweaks and options in every mode, and the most realistic animation of any Madden yet—and a way to pay respect to the man himself!

Whether you're looking to play through a player's career, play six-on-six games in The Yard, or build your own NFL Ultimate Team, *NFL 23* has you covered. What's more, EA Sports has made changes to Franchise mode that make it even more authentic. Looking for the ultimate football game? This is it!

QUICK TIPS

TRAIN UP
■ *NFL 23* has a bunch of control tweaks and new skills to learn, and they're worth learning. Use the Skills Trainer feature to get used to them, then hit them hard once you're on the field.

DIVE FOR DISTANCE
■ Diving can grab you some extra distance when you're carrying—or give you a last-ditch tackle when you're playing defense. Tap or press and hold the X or square button to launch yourself forward.

MOTIVATION
■ Signing players in Franchise mode was once all about the money, but in *NFL 23* they're motivated by other things as well, including their history with the club, their Super Bowl ambitions, and even the weather in the city where the team plays!

IT'S IN THE GAME!

■ *Madden NFL 23* brings some cool new additions to the modes and the game play, making it an even stronger gridiron game.

FieldSENSE

■ FieldSENSE is the name of *Madden's* new animation system, designed to give you more control in every position so that you can rush, tackle, block, and cover in a full 360-degree circle around the current player. It changes the whole feel of the game.

PASSING

■ Passing has also been revamped, with a new optional skill-based passing system where you need to press and hold the button to set the placement and accuracy. It's tough, but with practice you can pull off killer passes that give you more distance and control.

THE YARD

■ *Madden's* turbo-charged Casual football mode is back, giving you speedy six-on-six matches against other players and special challenge events. There's even an event based around SpongeBob SquarePants, played on its own Bikini Bottom–themed field!

PAYING TRIBUTE

■ By working with Electronic Arts on the *Madden* series, John Madden helped define what a sports game could be. It's only right that *NFL 23* pays tribute with a special match where two John Maddens coach each team from the touchline.

FAST FACT

Over forty different *Madden* games have appeared on different computers and consoles since the first *Madden* launched in 1988. The cover of the *NFL 23 All Madden Edition* is based on the original game's cover!

LIKE THIS? TRY THIS:

NHL 23

■ Prefer the ice to the football field? *NHL 23* is another amazing installment of the classic hockey game, with mixed women and men's teams in the Hockey Ultimate Team mode and new game play strategies.

FIFA 23

THE BEAUTIFUL GAME AT ITS BEST

People around the world call soccer "the beautiful game," and it's never looked or played better than in *FIFA 23*. While it's still flush with different modes and ways to play, EA Sports has gone back to fundamentals, rebuilding the way the game plays so that it's more exciting and more physical—just like the real deal! Whether you want to play in national or regional tournaments from around the world, follow your own soccer career, or play Volta street soccer with your friends, there's something here for you. And only in this final *FIFA* can you relive the thrills of the 2022 World Cup!

QUICK TIPS

PRACTICE YOUR PASSING

■ Passing is key to moving the ball up the field and creating opportunities to score a goal. Use the drills to get your head around ground passes and lobs until you've mastered all the passing skills.

SLOW DOWN YOUR DRIBBLE

■ Sprinting can get you near the goal fast, but when you need to get through the defense, slow things down. Pressing L1 or LB as you dribble will help you shield the ball from opposition players.

TAKE THE SHOT

■ You can modify your shots into Finesse, Flair, or Power shots by holding down the R1, L2, or R1 and L1 buttons as you shoot. The timing can be tricky, but you get a better chance of beating the goalie.

SERIOUS **SOCCER**

■ *FIFA 23* sets a new standard for realistic soccer, though not at the expense of fast-paced thrills and fun. EA Sports has gone to town with the graphics and animation, and changed the game play to make it even more authentic.

GETTING PHYSICAL

■ *FIFA's* animation captures the way players move and clash on the pitch. Different players now accelerate at different speeds in different ways, making fast, agile players tougher to defend against.

GUARD THE BALL

■ *FIFA* has gotten smarter about how it calculates where the ball will go when it's deflected, and what will happen when an attacking player comes into contact with a defender. It pays to dodge and weave through the defense, using your skills to guard the ball from interception.

LEAGUES AHEAD

■ For the first time, *FIFA 23* features women's soccer, including the UEFA Women's Champions League, the English Women's Super League, and France's Division 1 Féminine. There's no NWSL yet, but you can play with national women's teams from around the globe, including the USA.

PUT SOME POWER IN

■ The new Power Shots can make it easier to score in a crowded box, but they also leave your striker vulnerable to getting tackled. Move in fast and find clear space, though, and you can score some spectacular goals!

FAST FACT

FIFA 23 is the final *FIFA* as we know it, as EA Sports has fallen out with FIFA, the world soccer authority, and is starting up its own soccer franchise: *EA Sports FC*. Still, *FIFA 23* sees the series going out with the bang that it deserves!

LIKE THIS? **TRY THIS:**

KNOCKOUT CITY

■ Would you rather play dodgeball than soccer? *Knockout City* is a hypercharged game inspired by dodgeball, played online with up to eight players. It's fast-paced, easy to get into, and a blast to play.

NBA 2K23

Raise your game with the top dribbling, shooting, and defensive tips

I f *NBA 2K22* transformed *NBA 2K's* defensive game, *2K23* reworks how you shoot and how you dribble—and how you make your plays. There's a lot to learn, but if you find life tough on the court, don't worry. We've got the tips to turn you into a b-ball powerhouse!

1 Find space to shoot

■ The days of just running at the hoop or blasting out midrange shots are over. You need to make space and create opportunities. Pay attention to your teammates and look for holes in the defense. Make space for your own players, and use passing to keep the ball moving and stop defenders clogging up the paint. Instead of focusing on the shot, focus on making the plays that will get it through the hoop.

2 Play smart on defense

■ If the offense is about creating opportunities, defense is about shutting them down. Make sure your active player is guarding the assigned opposition player, but don't get too focused on following the guard arrow—react to what the defense is doing and fill in any spaces. You need to stop plays from building up.

FAST FACT

Michael Jordan isn't just one of the game's cover stars, but the subject of an awesome challenge mode where you can replicate his greatest plays in his most legendary games, complete with a range of cool vintage TV effects.

Don't force shots

3

■ There are times when you have to shoot quickly, but don't rush if you're under pressure from the defense. Trying to force a shot from a bad situation will only give the defense the ball, so hold back, use your time, watch the countdown, and try to make some space. If all else fails, go for a step-back move. Just flick the right analog stick down, then take your shot.

4

Upgrade your dribble

■ *NBA 2K23* switches things up so that you can't keep sprinting and dribbling forever. You now have three adrenaline boosts for high-speed dribbling, and one goes every time you sprint hard with the ball. They only get refilled when the shot clock resets. Instead of going fast, slow things down and use the controls. Try flicking the right stick up and down or left and right in a rhythm to try different dribbling combos.

Work on your shots

■ To score you need a tool bag full of shots for different situations. That means midrange shots, jump shots, dunks, finishers, and rebounds. That means mastering a lot of button combos, and you're only going to get that if you practice. Put in the time and get a feel for every shot. Here are a few to get you started.

JUMP SHOT: Press and hold X/Square, then release.

LAYUP: Move and hold the right stick up while driving.

RUNNER/FLOATER: Move and hold the right stick down while driving.

TWO-HAND DUNK: Hold R2 and move and hold the right stick up while driving.

FLASHY DUNK: Pull off a two-hand dunk, but release the right stick at the last second.

5

Prepare for rebounds

■ Instead of shooting and hoping for the best, assume that every shot will miss and get ready for the rebound. Try to anticipate where the ball will go and get there first. If you're a defender, getting between an offense player and the hoop can halt any follow-up play and put your team in possession of the ball. Press the left trigger to grab it. If you're on the offense, holding the X or Square button can put the ball back through the hoop.

FIGHT!

Call them beat-'em-ups, fighting games, or brawlers, they've been around for almost as long as we've had video games. Like the shoot-'em-up or the racing game, they started out in the arcades, first with primitive boxing games like Sega's *Heavyweight Champ* (1987), then with the first wave of karate and kung-fu games. *Karate Champ* (1984) set the scene, with two karate masters facing off across three hard-hitting rounds while a timer counted down. Then *Yie Ar Kung-Fu* shook things up by bringing in a series of enemies to defeat, each armed with a different kung-fu weapon.

The classic
Street Fighter II
in action

The original
fighter,
Karate Champ

■ These early hits inspired a wave of computer fighting games, including *Way of the Exploding Fist* (1985) and *International Karate* (1987). But the fighting game really got going with *Street Fighter* (1987): the first fighting game to take you on a dragon-punching, high-kicking tour around the world against a series of tough opponents.

■ The real breakthrough came with the sequel, *Street Fighter II* (1991), This was the first fighting game to feature a wider set of characters, each with their own special moves. Its ten world warriors—Ryu, Ken, Chun-Li, Dhalsim, Blanka, and the

rest—are still some of the best known and loved gaming characters around. *Street Fighter II* was also the first fighting game to launch new special editions featuring new fighters, new backgrounds, and new tweaks to the game play.

■ *Street Fighter II* was a massive success, becoming one of the top three biggest sellers of all time. It inspired dozens of imitators, and though some of them would disappear within a year or so— barely anyone remembers *Eternal Champions* (1993) or *World Heroes* (1992)—others would go on to become legends in their own right!

FIGHTING LEGEND: FATAL FURY

■ Released as *Legend of the Hungry Wolf* in Japan, SNK's mighty brawler was *Street Fighter II*'s biggest rival, probably because it was designed by Takashi Nishiyama, the creator of the original *Street Fighter*. *Fatal Fury* had a great lineup of fighters, including hero Terry Bogard and his crime lord enemy, Geese Howard, and some spectacular locations. It was the first in a wave of SNK hits, spawning the *Art of Fighting* and *King of Fighters* series.

1993

1991

FIGHTING LEGEND: SAMURAI SHOWDOWN

■ Another SNK classic, *Samurai Showdown* was one of the first fighting games to focus on weapons more than hand-to-hand combat. It took the action back to 18th-century Japan, with its Samurai warriors, ninjas, shrine maidens, and monsters battling with a range of swords, spears, claws, and daggers. The bloodshed was toned down for its US console release, but it set the stage for games like the *Soulcalibur* series and *Super Smash Bros*.

THE 3D ERA

■ In the early 1990s, the world's big arcade game manufacturers started experimenting with 3D graphics, and having made one of the first true 3D racing games, *Virtua Racer*, Sega went to work on the first true 3D fighting game. While its blocky characters look weird today, *Virtua Fighter* (1993) caused a sensation, and came out just as Sega and Sony were designing the first 3D games consoles. Sega released *Virtua Fighter* as a launch game for its Saturn console, while the PlayStation launched with its own 3D brawler, *Battle Arena Toshinden* (1995). However, Sony had its real *Virtua Fighter* rival waiting in the wings. Produced by Namco, *Tekken* hit the arcades in 1994 and launched on the PlayStation just a few months after its release. With its hard-hitting martial arts action and darker story lines, it was too good to ignore.

■ Together, *Tekken* and *Virtua Fighter* set the standard for 3D fighting games. They were still played much like 2D fighting games—your fighters couldn't move in and out of the screen—but the smoothly animated characters

FINAL 03'01"95
HEIHACHI PUSH SELECT

Tekken made fighting games cool

and spectacular 3D graphics got a new generation of players excited. While the PlayStation was making console gaming cool for a bigger audience, *Tekken* was doing the same for fighting games. Soon there were others, like the weapons-based *Soul Edge* (1995) and *Bushido Blade* (1997), or the dynamic *Dead or Alive* (1996). *Soul Edge* morphed into *Soulcalibur* (1998), starting another big series for Namco.

Capcom's classic X-Men fighting game

■ Still, the 2D fighter wasn't dead. Capcom kept producing competitive beat-'em-ups with better graphics, bigger champions, and awesome special effects. *Street Fighter Alpha* (1995) and *Street Fighter III* (1997) continued the *Street Fighter* legacy, while the *Darkstalkers* (1994) and *X-Men vs. Street Fighter* (1996) series combined fighting games with Gothic horror and superheroes. Meanwhile, *Super Smash Bros.* (1999) gave us a new kind of fighting game, where Nintendo's greatest heroes could battle it out in an arena of platforms, and you weren't knocked out until you were literally knocked off the stage!

Soulcalibur was another smash hit

Horror meets fighting in Darkstalkers

FIGHTING LEGEND: GUILTY GEAR

■ Through its *BlazBlue* and *Guilty Gear* series, Arc System Works has become famous with fighting game fans for making tough but beautiful 2D brawlers. *Guilty Gear* was its first big hit, wowing gamers with its smooth animation, tactical game play, and super-cool characters who looked like they'd stepped straight out of a Japanese cartoon. *Guilty Gear Strive* (2021) proves that the series still has what it takes today!

1998

FIGHTING LEGEND: POWERSTONE

■ One of the launch games for Sega's Dreamcast console, *PowerStone* was Capcom's attempt to make a real 3D fighting game. You could move and jump in every direction and pick up objects to throw at your opponent and weapons to wallop them with. *PowerStone*'s levels also had cool interactive scenery that could damage the fighters, really keeping players on their toes.

1999

THE BATTLE CONTINUES

■ As the PlayStation and Saturn gave way to new generations of consoles, the fighting game has gone from strength to strength. Capcom found a way to bring the worlds of 2D and 3D fighting games together with the incredible *Street Fighter IV* (2008) and *Marvel vs. Capcom 3* (2011), while Namco's *Tekken* and *Soulcalibur* series are still pushing out the hits.

■ Perhaps the most exciting thing about today's fighting games is that they cover a huge range of styles and themes. There are skills-focused fighters inspired by Japanese anime, like the *Guilty Gear* series (1998 to 2021) and *BlazBlue: Calamity Trigger* (2008). There are bombastic superhero brawlers, like *Injustice: Gods Among Us* (2013) and its sequel. We even get cool, 3D adaptations of the *Naruto* and *DragonBall Z* animated shows.

2D fighting at its best in *BlazBlue*

***BlazBlue* is always a blast from the past!**

Superhero scraps in *Injustice*

■ Even *Super Smash Bros.* has a wave of imitators, including *MultiVersus* (2022), *Brawlhalla* (2014), and *Nickelodeon All-Star Brawl* (2021). As long as there are players with the skills and energy to battle, there will always be amazing fighting games!

FIGHTING LEGEND: STREET FIGHTER IV

■ The series that started it all seemed to be losing its way before Capcom unleashed the incredible *Street Fighter IV*. This was the game that brought the fantasy cartoon style of the classic 2D fighting games into the world of modern 3D graphics, then mixed things up with furiously fast-paced combat and the greatest lineup of champs ever seen. The legend was reborn!

2008

FIGHTING CULTURE

■ Almost as soon as *Street Fighter II* and *Fatal Fury* hit the arcades, a loyal community of fans grew up around the fighting game. They would play winner-stays-on matches for hours in arcades from Los Angeles to London to Tokyo, developing killer strategies and working out which in-game champions had the edge on their rivals.

■ These days the culture has moved to the internet and the competition is mostly online, but the fighting game community is as enthusiastic as ever. Every year there are major online and offline tournaments, with the biggest—the Evolution Championship Series (known as Evo)—attracting millions of viewers, with the finals playing out in huge arenas in Las Vegas and Tokyo.

FIGHTING TALK

■ Like many other types of game, fighting games have developed their own language, which explains how different parts of the games work and the different strategies players use. Want to get involved? You'd better master these terms and more:

Bait: A move you use to encourage your opponent to try a risky move, leaving them open to your counter.

Blockstun: The length of time a character is unable to move while they're blocking an attack.

Combo: A string or chain of attacks. An air combo is a combo of attacks you pull off in the air.

Counter: A move that blocks an incoming attack and hits your opponent with an attack of your own.

Cancel: A move that cancels your previous move so that you can try something else and catch your opponent out.

Dash: A move that takes you toward or away from your opponent at high speed, getting you into battle or away from an incoming blow.

Frame Advantage: The advantage you get when your last move takes less time to recover from than your opponent's, giving you the chance to hit or dodge with your next move first.

Hitbox: The parts of one character that can hit or be hit by another character. These can be bigger or smaller than the character you see on the screen.

Safe and Unsafe: Safe moves are fast moves that don't leave you open to attack. Unsafe moves are risky moves that do more damage but give your opponent the chance to get a fast attack in first.

TEKKEN 8

Behold the ultimate fighting game!

Street Fighter 6 looks awesome, but Bandai Namco's latest is "tekken" the fighting game to a whole new level. It's tekken names and kicking bottoms. It's tekken *Mortal Kombat* to the cleaners and is leaving *Killer Instinct* in the dust.

This one's got it all: *Tekken*'s classic, hard-hitting combat, one of the best rosters of any fighting game and—arguably—the most advanced graphics in the whole fighting genre, thanks to the Unreal 5.0 engine. When fist meets fate in *Tekken 8*, it will knock your eyes into the back of your skull (book a doctor's appointment in advance).

■ Moving to the new Unreal 5.0 engine has allowed Bandai Namco's artists to put more detail into the game than ever before. Muscles tense and flex with great realism, while faces are the most expressive they've ever been. If you want to watch characters grimace in anger or the pain of being pummeled, this is the game for you!

■ Of course, it's not just Jin and Kazuya trading blows in combat! Everyone wants a piece of the action. King, Paul Phoenix, Marshall Law, Jack-8, and Jun Kazama are all coming back for another bust-up—and they're joined by some old favorites and new recruits.

■ Like any great *Tekken*, the story centers on the struggles of the Mishima clan, with young Jin and his dad, Kazuya, on opposite sides of the ongoing Devil Gene war. In this family there's only one way to settle an argument: a huge fight!

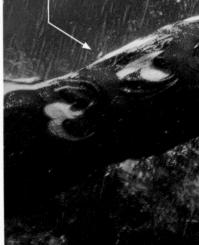

FAST FACT

Tekken, which means "iron fist" in Japanese, is so popular in Japan that there's a museum dedicated to it at Namco's Sugamo arcade in Tokyo. Entry is free and you can check out *Tekken* memorabilia, trophies, arcade games, and more.

■ *Tekken 8* goes big on dramatic weather effects and epic animated backgrounds. Storms will rage, lightning will crash, and enormous ships will be ripped into pieces. It will get messy—and it will look cool.

MULTIVERSUS

Top tips to get you started in this mighty fighting game

MultiVersus is a treat for fans of superheroes, toons, and fighting games. It's got an amazing roster of characters and brilliant game play—and it's free to play! It is, however, a tricky platform fighter, even if you've played *Super Smash Bros.* and *Nickelodeon All-Star Brawl*. Don't panic! We've got the hints and tips to help you master *MultiVersus*.

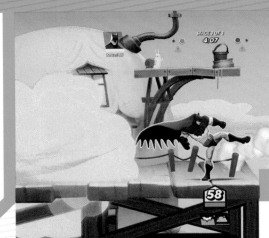

Learn one fighter first

■ Find a character you like and stick to them in the early stages. You'll learn their moves in more depth and work out whether they're strongest on the horizontals (across the platforms) or the verticals (smashing enemies into the sky). Most importantly, you'll gain Mastery Levels with that character and start unlocking perks. It's good to get to grips with other characters— you'll understand their weaknesses—but concentrate on learning one at first.

Use your perks

■ Perks are really useful. You can have four in action at any time— with three generic perks and one signature perk—and each will give you useful buff to increase damage, boost your defenses, or help you support your team. Hit Mastery Level 9 and you can even "train" your fighter to learn another fighter's perks. Work out which perks support your play style and use them.

FAST FACT

Velma can lose her glasses in *MultiVersus* when she crawls along the ground. Check out what happens to the screen if she does— it made us chuckle.

Dodge to survive

■ You can't block in *MultiVersus*, which makes your dodge move the best way out of trouble. You can use it to avoid incoming attacks or cancel a power move you're building; you can even use them when you're in the air. The dodge meter means you can't dodge endlessly, but if you're mixing dodges with attacks, that won't be a problem.

Watch your position

■ *MultiVersus* is all about knocking your opponents off the screen while avoiding getting knocked out yourself. That means watching to make sure that you're not vulnerable to a massive thump that could send you flying, and exploiting any opening your opponent gives you to smash them sideways or upward to their doom. Try to avoid getting caught near the edge, top, or bottom of the map, and guard the edges when an opponent has been knocked off to stop them reaching safety. Sometimes you need to take a risk and jump off after them to knock them out for good!

Fight as a team

■ Co-op matches are brilliant fun, but you need to learn how to fight as part of a team. Watch your teammate, help them when they're getting weak, and don't be shy about ganging up on a weakened foe. It also helps if you know each fighter's role. Tanks soak up damage, while Assassins dish it out. Mages are good for attacking from a safe distance. Bruisers give you a balance of offensive and defensive skills, while Support characters have abilities that can keep teammates in the fight. Learn your role, work together, and you'll win.

Decays and cooldowns

■ The makers of *MultiVersus* don't want you to spam the same overpowered attacks. That's why some of your best special moves have cooldowns. Learn how long these last and save those moves for when you need them. You're also hit by an Attack Decay effect if you keep using the same attack. This makes the attack much less powerful, so mix up your moves if you want to win the battle.

113

WWE 2K23

The best is back with extra Cena!

■ John Cena isn't just the cover superstar of the latest *WWE 2K*—he's also the focus of an updated Showcase game mode covering the biggest moments of his incredible twenty-year career. And that's not all the new *WWE* has going for it, with more modes, story lines, and wrestling heroes than any *WWE* before!

You can't see me

■ The John Cena Showcase mode features fourteen of the WWE icon's most exciting matches, running from his Hot Summer Night debut in 2002 to his gripping 2021 SummerSlam battle against Roman Reigns. Expect to see some of the WWE's mightiest champions along the way!

FAST FACT

WWE 2K23 isn't the first game in the series with a superstar Showcase mode. *WWE 2K22* featured Rey Mysterio, while *WWE 2K15* had a DLC pack starring Ultimate Warrior. *WWE 2K19* followed Daniel Bryan in the ring, while *WWE 2K16* had a special Showcase starring Stone Cold Steve Austin himself.

Never give up . . .

■ Instead of focusing on Cena's victories, the Showcase gives you matches where Cena loses. Can he embrace his "never give up" spirit, pick himself up from the mat and win, or will you, as one of his notorious opponents, stop him rewriting the story?

Master of the Universe

■ Want to run your own take on the WWE? The revamped Universe mode puts you in control. Manage your wrestlers, create your own rivalries, and program your own weekly shows and major live events. The level of detail is incredible, down to how matches start, and how the usual seasonal feuds play out.

Rise and shine!

■ The MyRISE mode returns revamped with different story lines for the men's and women's divisions, following the journey of a WWE star from rookie first-timer to legendary champ. And if you'd prefer, you can still run your own team in the MyFACTION mode—and take it out to battle other teams online!

WarGames

■ Two teams in two rings, surrounded by a chain-link fence. When you're in the middle of the carnival of carnage that is WarGames, it's tough work just making it out in one piece! The team at Visual Concepts has used the power of the Xbox Series S/X and PS5 to build the most ambitious WWE mode ever, with new ways to move around and between the two rings to trash the opposition.

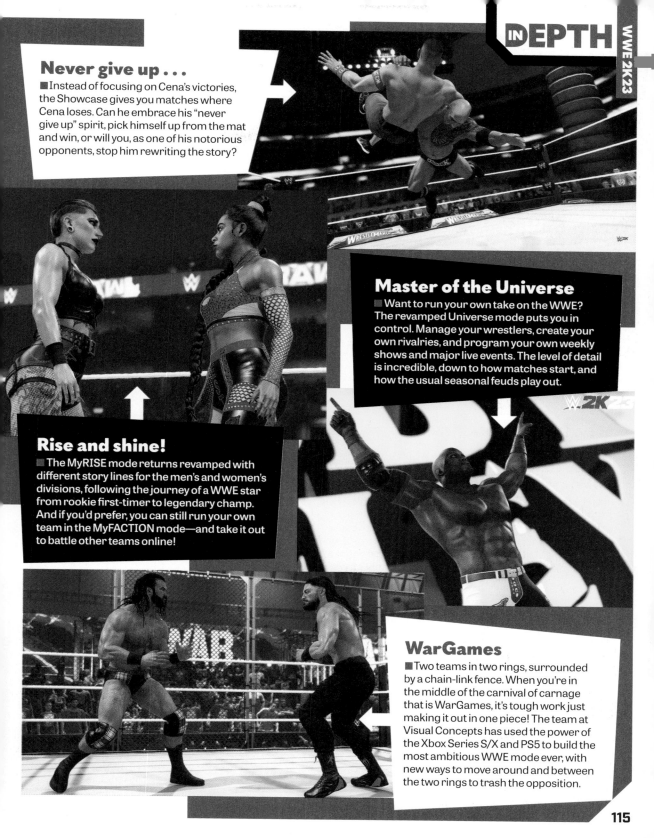

Crash Team Rumble

Two squads clash in the ultimate Bandicoot brawl!

■ Crash and his chums are back, but this time there's no platforming or racing. Nope, this time, they're ready to rumble. The Bandicoot's latest is a team-based, multiplayer action game, where two squads of four battle across impressive, multilevel maps to snag maximum quantities of Wumpa fruit and deliver them back to their goal. With an epic lineup of fan-favorite heroes and villains, you've got a fiercely competitive game that's a whole lot of fun!

Meet the contenders

■ You already know most of the star players. Crash and his sister Coco lead the roster, followed by series villains, the Doctors Neo Cortex, Nitrus Brio, and Nefarious Tropy. Loyal goon Dingodile is there for muscle, along with Crash's crush, Tawna. Each character has their own distinct abilities and play style.

Wild arenas
■ Each 4v4 match takes place across a wild island arena, with the Wumpa fruit spread out around multiple levels and zones. You'll still need your awesome platforming skills to reach the fruit first and get it to your goal.

FAST FACT

The first *Crash Bandicoot* had a hidden level—Stormy Ascent—that was too difficult to be made part of the original game. It could be accessed using cheats, but only became fully playable with the release of the *N. Sane Trilogy* remaster.

Blast and brawl
■ Gathering the Wumpa fruit is one thing. Holding on to it is something else! Luckily, every hero or villain has their own weapons, moves, and abilities, perfect for whacking your foes and relieving them of their harvest, or keeping the opposing team off your teammates' back. That's why they call it a rumble!

Score big!
■ To win, you'll need to get your fruit to your team's goal and bank it, while battling the other team for possession of the goodies and key control points. There's no time to stand around in this wild all-star scrap. You need to get out there, out-collect, and out-fight the other team—and win the match!

TOP 10

THE BEST MOBILE GAMES

Gaming on the go? These are the hot picks to download.

10 Streets of Rage 4

■ *Streets of Rage* was THE scrolling beat-'em-up when your mom and dad were kids, and this fourth game in the series should give you some idea why. Just like in the old days, an evil crime syndicate has taken control of the streets, and the only way to stop them is to take out every punk, thug, crooked cop, and gang enforcer in hand-to-hand combat. From the retro cartoon graphics to the nonstop action, this does justice to the original classics while packing in some cool new secrets on the way.

AVAILABLE ON: iOS, Android

09 League of Legends: Wild Rift

■ *Wild Rift* does a fantastic job of taking the classic *League* game play and shrinking it down to mobile size. You can pick from an awesome selection of ninety-five champions pulled straight out of the main game, and get to business in 5v5 battles that kick off at a furious pace. *Wild Rift* still rewards high skills and brilliant strategy, while regular updates keep the action challenging and fun. Sure, you can find other mobile MOBA games, but why bother when you can play the best?

AVAILABLE ON: iOS, Android

08 Descenders

■ *Descenders* was a hit on console, and it's just as good on your phone! Whether you're speeding down a gnarly mountain track or making your way across extreme stunt courses, the superb controls give you a fighting chance of staying in the saddle. What's more, the courses change each time you play, so you're never stuck trying to make the same jump over and over. With rep to build, bikes to unlock, and teams to join, don't be surprised if you can't put it down.

AVAILABLE ON: iOS, Android

WHERE'S THE GIRL? SHE WAS SUPPOSED TO WAIT HERE!

07 Dungeons of Dreadrock

■ There are dozens of dungeon crawlers styled after the classic *Legend of Zelda* games, but *Dungeons of Dreadrock* beats them all with a game that's less about fighting and exploring, and more about mind-bending puzzles. There are 100 sneaky puzzle levels to complete, all part of a story that will have you hooked, and each is packed with deadly traps and fiendish monsters. If you want a great adventure that will exercise your brain cells, give *Dreadrock* and its creepy caves a go.

AVAILABLE ON: iOS, Android

06 Genshin Impact

■ *Genshin* keeps getting better, and when you're not playing it on your console, you can grab your phone and play it on the road! In the past year, miHoYo has added new heroes to adventure with and huge new areas to explore, taking the story in exciting new directions, while the mix of quests, exploration, and real-time battles never gets tired. Whether you're loafing in the Lokapala Jungle or fighting through The Chasm, Teyvat is the place to be.

AVAILABLE ON: iOS, Android

04 Total War Battles: Warhammer

■ Finally, you can have all the excitement and strategy of the brilliant tabletop wargame on your tablet or smartphone. *Total War Battles* takes its game play from the classic PC *Total War: Warhammer* series, focusing in on epic conflicts that see massive armies meeting for a rumble. With orcs, elves, goblins, dwarves, and rat-like skaven to battle, you can expect some wild units on the field, and it all looks unbelievably good—if your device can handle all that action.

AVAILABLE ON: iOS, Android

05 T3 Arena

■ Saying that *T3 Arena* is a clone of *Overwatch* is putting it mildly, but it is a very good one. It's a 3v3 hero shooter where you can play with friends or go solo, with a good selection of straight deathmatch, escort, and control point modes and a strong roster of champions. The heroes all have their own spectacular specials and unbelievable ultimates, just like *Overwatch*'s stars, and the slick visuals and smooth controls make this the closest thing on mobile to Blizzard's mighty banger.

AVAILABLE ON: iOS, Android

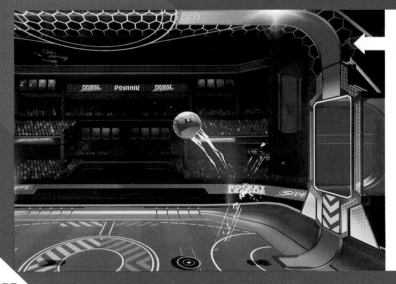

03 Rocket League Sideswipe

■ *Rocket League* has been crying out for a mobile version, and with *Sideswipe* it finally got it. Two-minute matches keep the action intense, especially with another three players on the pitch, and you can still pull off trick shots and bonkers freestyle stunts thanks to the easy touch controls. The 2D action makes it easy to get into, but it still has the depth for hardcore fans, with seasonal rankings and plenty of ways to make your car your own. Don't miss the brilliant seasonal modes!

AVAILABLE ON: iOS, Android

02 Final Fantasy VII: Ever Crisis

■ *Final Fantasy VII Remake* gave us a new vision of the most legendary *Final Fantasy*, but it's not the only way to enjoy this classic story. *Ever Crisis* does an incredible job of bringing it to your phone or tablet, mixing an updated version of the original's graphics with slick illustrations and turn-based combat using the newer *Remake* characters. It even fits in the stories from the spin-off games *Before Crisis*, *Dirge of Cerberus*, and *Crisis Core*.

AVAILABLE ON: iOS, Android

Cloud   5530/5530

Braver   Armor Break   Raikiri   Fira Blow   Ruinra   Attack

01 Marvel Snap

■ Sorry, *Hearthstone*, *Yu-Gi-Oh*, and *Legends of Runeterra*—there is a new king of mobile card games in town! *Marvel Snap* keeps its matches fast and thrilling, with just six rounds and a deck that only holds twelve cards. Games finish in just a few minutes, and even when you lose, there's some new card or upgrade to look forward to. Most importantly, you don't have to pay to have fun. Master the game and you'll keep finding new cards and strategies—and the confidence to gamble on a Snap!

AVAILABLE ON: iOS, Android

FAST FACT

Marvel Snap is the first game from Second Dinner, a studio set up by two *Hearthstone* developers, Ben Brode and Hamilton Chu. The studio is named after the second dinner the two used to have together after work, where they planned their escape into indie games!

CARD ART VARIANT SAMPLES

CAPTAIN MARVEL   CAPTAIN MARVEL   CAPTAIN MARVEL — AFTER THE FINAL TURN, MOVE TO A LOCATION THAT WINS YOU THE GAME. (IF POSSIBLE)   CAPTAIN MARVEL   CAPTAIN MARVEL

KERBAL SPACE PROGRAM 2

THIS TIME THEY'RE GOING INTERSTELLAR!

They say that games aren't rocket science, but—actually—*Kerbal Space Program 2* is. Take away the cute green Kerbals and their lovable antics, and there's a serious commitment to real-world astrophysics and engineering at the heart of this awesome space exploration game. Using concepts and data from the latest space research, the team at Intercept Games has simulated a huge range of starship parts and different engines to deliver some seriously scientific missions, and this time the Kerbals are going to an even farther frontier, to boldly go where no Kerbal has ever gone before!

QUICK TIPS

PICK YOUR ENGINE
■ Don't just go for the most powerful engine when you're putting your spacecraft together. Make sure you understand your mission, and choose the engine that will go the distance at the right speed.

PRACTICE YOUR EVA
■ Sometimes you need to get outside your vehicle, but using your jet pack isn't any kind of cakewalk. Get some practice in before you head out on the mission, or your Kerbals might not make it back home!

STICK TO EASY
■ While it's a little easier on new players than the first *Kerbal Space Program*, the sequel can still be a tough game to learn. Play on easy difficulty and it's more forgiving, providing your Kerbal astronauts with a fighting chance.

EXPLORING STRANGE NEW WORLDS

■ Kerbal science has progressed since the original *Kerbal Space Program*, and that means our Kerbal space explorers can go beyond the limits of the Kerbol System and reach planets orbiting the nearest stars. It's a whole new era for space travel!

READY FOR LAUNCH

■ Just getting off the launchpad can be a challenge, but *Kerbal Space Program 2* makes it easier to assemble your rockets and spacecraft and understand how your changes will make taking off easier or harder.

NEW ENGINE TECH

■ The sequel also features a wider range of engines and technology, covering everything from the high-powered rockets you'll need to leave gravity behind to deep-space engines capable of traveling over the vast distances between star systems.

RIDE THE ROVER

■ Of course, there's a lot of fun to be had just exploring the planets within your own Kerbol System. Why not take your rover on a mission to gather new resources, or find the right spot for a new colony?

MADE IN SPACE

■ Even the latest Kerbal space technology won't get you from Planet Kerbin to the farthest planets in one jump. That's why you can now build orbital docks and planetary colonies, where you can build new spacecraft to go even farther.

FAST FACT

The game's Kerbol System has five planets and two dwarf planets orbiting its sun, but is much smaller than our solar system. Our own Earth would orbit beyond the system's outer dwarf planet, Eeloo.

LIKE THIS? TRY THIS:

NO MAN'S SKY

■ Looking for a wilder take on space exploration? *No Man's Sky* has a whole universe of planets to discover, crammed with action, adventure, and mystery. It's the rare game that keeps on getting better.

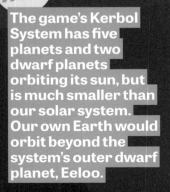

SLIME RANCHER II

Struggling to get your slime ranch started? We've got the tips to help.

Slime Rancher II looks cute, for sure, but there's a lot going on beneath the surface. Fail to get your slimes under control and keep 'em happy, and you're not going to make it as a rancher. The in-game help covers all the basics, but there are still some things you might not figure out straightaway. Check out our top six slime-keeping tips.

1

Wall 'em in

■ The single-level slime corrals might be fine for just a few slimes, but pack them in with too many slimes and they'll start jumping out. You'll also get rogue slimes and Largos busting in. That's why we'd recommend High Walls as an early upgrade. It will help you keep your slimes separate. Certain slimes will also need specific walls to keep them safe. Unless you keep Phosphor Slimes in a cave, upgrade to the Solar Shield walls.

FAST FACT

The way slimes will stack and climb on top of each other to escape your corral wasn't intentional in the first *Slime Rancher*, but the developers liked it so much that they made it a feature!

2

Get farming

■ Gathering food for your slimes takes a lot of time, so why not grow it yourself in the conservatory? Turn one or more of your plots into a Garden, then feed fruit or veg into the depositor. Either a tree will instantly grow with more fruit on the way, or you'll have a vegetable bed growing much-needed slime food. You can harvest from there and take it straight to your slimes.

Favorite foods

3

■ Each type of slime will only eat one type of food—except the Pink Slime, which eats just about everything! All other slimes also have a favorite meal, releasing twice the Plorts when they eat it. Try giving Water Lettuce to the Cotton Slimes or Cuberry to the Phosphor Slimes, and you'll get a lot more Plorts out of them.

4

Feed the Gordos

■ When you wander around, you'll meet Gordos—massive slimes that stay rooted to the spot. You can't move them, but you can feed them. Give them enough food and they'll burst, releasing more slimes into the area and unlocking fast routes to new locations. Feeding Gordos is the fastest way to see more of Rainbow Island.

Learn about Largos

■ Slimes produce a little nugget of Plort every time they eat, which you can sell for credit. If a slime of one type eats another type's Plort, it turns into a bigger, bunny-eared Largo. This isn't all bad—Largos can jump higher and farther, and you can't suck them up with your Vacpack, but they also produce more Plorts when fed. However, if they eat a Plort of a third type, they can transform into a Tarr slime. These guys won't just try to eat all the other slimes—they'll also have a go at eating you!

Explore and expand

5

■ Don't spend too much time in the conservatory. Get out and explore the island! You'll find new slimes you can only find in some locations, and new foods to feed them with. You'll also find new minerals to harvest, enabling you to put together new upgrades for your suit and Vacpack. You can also expand the conservatory by paying to unlock new areas. You'll need them to corral and feed all your new slime friends!

125

TWO POINT CAMPUS

If there's anything we've learned from Two Point's management games, it's to expect the unexpected. *Two Point Hospital* jumped off the rails with its weird illnesses and ridiculous treatments. Now *Two Point Campus* gives us a college management sim where monsters might stalk the campus corridors or you could end up running a school for chefs, witches and wizards, or spies!

Whatever your college is teaching, you know you're going to be busy. With specialist classrooms to build along with college dorms and student facilities, you need to spend your budgets wisely—and that's without hiring janitors and teachers. Luckily, the game does a great job of easing you in and making life on campus fun. Keep your students happy and passing their exams, and you'll conquer every challenge in your way.

QUICK TIPS

DON'T WASTE YOUR KUDOSH
■ You need Kudosh to unlock new furniture and gadgets, but don't spend it without thinking. Save some back for crucial items or it will have a big impact on your students or teachers.

TAKE CARE OF YOUR STUDENTS
■ Dorms, beds, bathrooms, and shower rooms are a must, but don't forget about libraries with study spaces, student unions, clubs, and common rooms. Happy students with the right resources mean better grades.

ONE TO ONE
■ Some students need more hands-on teaching time than others, so make sure you've got a private tuition space and enough teachers to man it. It could turn a failing student into a future graduate!

126

TOO COOL FOR SCHOOL

■ There's a lot to manage in *Two Point Campus*. The courses are bizarre, the staff can be lazy, the students aren't always the brightest sparks, and you need to keep the grades going up and everyone smiling.

KITCHEN NIGHTMARES

■ At this college you're teaching a new generation of chefs. You'll need to train them to make sensational mains and desserts if you want your star chefs to win a cook-off. Still, you've got the gadget-packed kitchens to do it!

PLAY IT LOUD!

■ Campus events can boost your students' happiness and improve their movement speed and motivation. Why not schedule in a talent show, movie, or party—or book a new band to play their latest hits?

FROM HARVARD TO HOGWARTS

■ It's not hard to work out what inspired this school of witches and wizardry. The Spiffinmore Academy is in trouble. Can you teach your students the magical skills they'll need to survive haunted classrooms, dark sorcery, and ancient curses?

KEEPING TRACK

■ The secret of success is making sure that staff and students get everything they need. You can click on a student, janitor, teacher, or assistant and find out how they feel or what they want. Maybe some time in the library or a chance to unwind could help them do better?

FAST FACT

It's no accident that Two Point Studios' games have the same style and British humor you'd find in the classics *Theme Hospital* and *Fable*. Many of the team worked at legendary studios like Bullfrog Productions and Lionhead, helping to make the original games!

LIKE THIS? TRY THIS:

TWO POINT HOSPITAL

■ Two Point's first game is a spiritual successor to the awesome *Theme Hospital*, going big on gruesome but funny made-up illnesses, daft treatments, and silly gags. Sickness has never been so much fun!

HI-FI RUSH

BECOME A ROBOT-WRECKING ROCK GOD!

Hi-Fi Rush is the sci-fi beat-'em-up action game that's all about the beats. As wannabe rockstar Chai, you've volunteered for an experimental treatment that's left you with a robot arm and an old-school music player in your chest. The evil corporation behind it is now calling you a defect and has sentenced you to death. There's only one way to defeat this system: smash and bash your way through an army of robots and take on their horrible bosses.

Causing mayhem with your mighty axe will get you somewhere, but to max out the damage you've got to hit them on the beat. Switch up your rhythms to pull off combos, and you can take on the world and win!

QUICK TIPS

For some people, the beat is hard to find, like inner peace, but here are some tips!

GET THE HINT

■ Talk to the hint robots you'll find around the levels. They can teach you new techniques and combos, and you'll get a chance to try them out.

USE THE GRAPPLE

■ Your robot arm's grapple is more than just a way to get from A to B. You can also use it to grapple onto robots and hit them faster, making it easier to keep chaining your attacks.

VISUALIZE THE BEAT

■ Struggling to match the rhythm? Press the View button on your Xbox controller to see a scrolling bar that marks every beat. Lights, machines, and billboards will also pulse in time.

APPETITE FOR DESTRUCTION

■ You're not the first "defect" that Vandelay Technologies has tried to eliminate, but you're going to make sure that you're one of the last. Legions of robots stand in your way, but you've got the tools to trash 'em. All it takes is a sense of rhythm and a little help from some newfound friends.

FEEL THE BEAT
■ Swing your axe in time with the music to build up your grade and dish out more damage. When the circles appear, time your next hit for when they overlap to maximize the impact.

MIX IT UP
■ For the maximum A and S grades, you need to switch between single-beat light attacks and two-beat heavies, chaining them together, or resting for a beat to pull off supercharged combos.

TAKE 'EM DOWN
■ Keep battling for what's right and you're going to come up against Vandelay's worst. If you think mega-robot QA-1MIL is bad enough, wait until you fight his cyborg boss, Rekka.

TAKE IT EASY
■ You can chill between missions at your new friend Peppermint's secret base. Here you can shop for upgrades or hang out with her robot cat, 808.

FAST FACT
Hi-Fi Rush isn't the sort of game you'd expect from its developer, Tango Gameworks. Before this, the studio was best known for seriously scary games like *Ghostwire: Tokyo* and *The Evil Within*!

LIKE THIS? TRY THIS:

BOMB RUSH CYBERFUNK
■ *Hi-Fi Rush* owes a lot to Sega classic *Jet Set Radio*, and the same goes for *Bomb Rush Cyberfunk*. With its skateboards, sci-fi setting, street gangs, and graffiti, it's a furiously stylish ride.

Park Beyond

These rides defy the laws of physics!

■ *Park Beyond* is a theme park sim with a difference. Like the old *RollerCoaster Tycoon* and *Planet Coaster* games, you have to develop great theme parks, fill them with rides, and design your own awesome roller coasters. But in *Park Beyond*, you don't have to obey the thrill-ride-ruining laws of gravity. Instead, impress your visitors and fill them with amazement, and you can "impossify" your rides to make them even more incredible. How about roller coasters with jumps, or a spinning octopus ride with extra-special tentacles? You can create these things and build the theme park paradise of your dreams!

Build amazement

■ Impossification doesn't come out of nowhere. You have to build up some "amazement" by adding rides that thrill your visitors, themed scenery that blows their minds, and food, drink, and merch stalls that satisfy all their cravings.

FAST FACT

The original *RollerCoaster Tycoon* and its sequel created an army of coaster-hungry fans. Some became roller coaster designers, while one fan spent a decade building his dream virtual theme park.

Kooky coasters
■ While most rides come ready-made, you're free to design and build any roller coaster that your brains and budget will allow. Put in hills, drops, loops, twists, and cobra rolls, or even kick-start your coaster with a launcher. The sky's the limit!

Impossify it!
■ With impossification you can take it even further. How about a cannon that blasts your coaster cars across a gap in the track, or tracks that switch as you loop the loop? Sure, in the real world this would end in disaster, but that's what impossification is all about!

Dream the impossible
■ As you go on, your crack team of designers, artists, and engineers will come up with even more ridiculous thrill rides that go from normal to supernatural in a New York minute. Why stick with one big wheel when you can stack another one right on top?

Suckers for punishment
■ You can impossify other rides, too. You've probably spun around on an octopus ride at a fun fair, but have you ever ridden one that tosses the cars around from one tentacle to another? These riders are either going to be pumped or feeling pretty sick!

MOONBREAKER

TAKING BATTLING FIGURES TO A WHOLE NEW LEVEL

★ **Extilior**

Methedori
Unranked

Melee

Captain

Rally
A random ally within range gains Shield of Hope when a rival is destroyed.

Shield of Hope
Reduce next damage to unit by 1

Sword of Justice
Deal 3 damage to ALL units in range.

We've seen plenty of video games based on tabletop battle games, but *Moonbreaker* takes things one step further. It's a digital miniatures strategy game where the characters really are virtual figures. You can move your troops around and command them to fight—and even paint them if that's your thing!

Win your battles, and you can build up a collection, paint 'em in your own style, and then take on your friends online. It's all the fun of a tabletop battle game, but with added special effects for all the action and the kind of scenery that most of us could never make!

QUICK TIPS

SHIELD THE CAPTAIN
■ Your captain is your most powerful unit, but if they die, your game is lost. Use them to dish out damage, but don't leave them exposed to enemy fire or hard-hitting melee attacks.

SAVE YOUR CINDER
■ You need Cinder to summon units from your bridge and activate your special moves, but you only get three per turn. Save some to summon heroes or use a killer move.

FIND COVER
■ Units with ranged weapons need to see you to hit you, so keep any weaker units or your Captain behind cover before your turn ends. The less chance they have of hitting you, the better.

COLLECT, PAINT, AND BATTLE

■ *Moonbreaker* doesn't have a traditional campaign with a story to follow, but who cares when you can build up your own perfect squad of warriors, get them looking good, and lead them into combat!

BUILD YOUR SQUAD
■ Before you can fight, you need to select a Captain and up to nine other units. Make sure you get a balance between low-cost units that won't cost you too much Cinder to deploy, and the bigger, tougher stars.

STRENGTHS AND WEAKNESSES
■ Each unit has its own strengths, weak spots, and abilities. If you want to be a *Moonbreaker* master, you need to learn what these are and how to use them. Some units have abilities that can support other units, or move them faster, so try out different strategies.

PAINT YOUR FIGURES
■ Why not make your roster your own? You can repaint any miniature in the game using an incredibly cool set of tools. These actually simulate the way that real-world painters work on figures, using a dry brush to apply highlights or a wash to create shadow effects. You can even swap your paint jobs with other players!

GROW YOUR SKILLS
■ Other players will provide your biggest challenge, but you don't need to take them on straightaway. You can practice against computer-controlled opponents or take on a Cargo Run. Here you fight against a series of captains. Have you got what it takes to keep fighting?

FAST FACT

Moonbreaker comes from Unknown Worlds—the team that brought us ace aquatic survival sim *Subnautica*. Its world and story were partly created by famous fantasy author Brandon Sanderson.

LIKE THIS? TRY THIS:

XCOM 2
■ While it's a more traditional turn-by-turn strategy game, *XCOM 2* is still a thriller, with humankind facing off against an alien menace in a story line full of action and drama.

133

Gotham Knights

Four heroes, one family, one mission

SPOILER ALERT! Batman dies at the start of *Gotham Knights*. So who's going to defend the city from its biggest crime wave ever? Nightwing, Batgirl, Robin, and the Red Hood—that's who! Bruce Wayne's nearest and dearest are getting the gang back together, to bring justice back to the streets of Gotham and solve the mystery behind the Dark Knight's final case.

Nightwing
(Dick Grayson)

■ The original Robin, Dick Grayson, ditched his sidekick status years ago to become a masked vigilante in his own right. He's a master acrobat and an expert in close combat, taking down Gotham's thugs with his dual escrima sticks.

HOW TO PLAY HIM:

Nightwing's fighting style is all about the acrobatics. Keep him moving from opponent to opponent, and build up momentum for his special attacks. Knock down enemies where you can and use heavy attacks to deal with armored foes. In co-op, use your heal and revive abilities to bring your teammates back to life.

Batgirl (Barbara Gordon)

■ The daughter of the legendary police commissioner Jim Gordon, Barbara Gordon is a high-tech genius, previously helping Batman battle crime with her hacking and surveillance skills as Oracle. Now back on the streets of Gotham as Batgirl, she's using her speed, smarts, and high-tech weapons to find out what's really going on.

HOW TO PLAY HER:

Batgirl has a cool mix of stealth abilities and offensive gadgets. Her extending Tonfa baton is one of the most flexible weapons in the game, with some hard-hitting combos and speedy attacks. Use her batarangs and hacking skills to disrupt and hamper groups of enemies, and use her Second Wind ability to revive yourself when you're in trouble.

Red Hood
(Jason Todd)

■ The second Robin, Jason Todd, was killed by the Joker and resurrected in a Lazarus Pit. His murderous rage turned him into the vengeful vigilante known as the Red Hood. Todd still has trouble holding his fury in check, but as a loyal member of the Batman family, he's now committed to staying on the right side of justice. He's Gotham's ultimate crime-fighting warrior.

HOW TO PLAY HIM:

There's no need to hold back or fight smart as Red Hood. He's a straight-up brawler, capable of dishing out huge damage with his melee attacks, dual pistols, and superpowered grapple moves. You've got more ranged firepower than any other hero and can punch through a gang of Gotham thugs before they know what hit 'em.

FAST FACT

Jason Todd died in the notorious *A Death in the Family* comic series, where a telephone vote from readers sealed the second Robin's fate. They voted for Todd to be killed off by the Joker, but he was resurrected 16 years later as Red Hood in the *Under the Hood* story line.

Robin (Tim Drake)

■ The latest hero to take the Robin name, Tim Drake finds it harder than his Bat family brethren to go it alone without the Batman. He has no reason to lack confidence, though, as his detective skills and grasp of strategy are second to none. With his quarterstaff, he can become an expert fighter, and he's the stealthiest hero of the bunch.

HOW TO PLAY HIM:

Use Robin's stealth skills wherever you can. In a close-up fight against overwhelming numbers, you're not going to last, but use high vantage points and the shadows to ambush your opponents, and you can bring those numbers down one by one. Smoke bombs and decoys can also even the odds, while investing in elemental attacks and teleport powers can turn Gotham's youngest knight into a mighty force for good.

MARVEL SNAP

Unlucky at Marvel's superpowered card game? We can help!

Marvel Snap is like many classic card games—easy to pick up, but more challenging to master. To win beyond the lowest levels, you'll need skill, strategy, and some real deck-building knowledge. Don't get mad if you're struggling, though. We've got some basic tips and tricks to help you win.

FAST FACT

Marvel Snap has a hidden system of pools that controls which cards you unlock. The second pool opens up when you reach collection level 214, where you'll be up against stronger players with even stronger cards.

1

Focus your strategy

■ You've got six rounds and three locations, so trying to win all three will get you nowhere. Instead, remember that you only need to win two locations, and focus on getting those. Sometimes you'll need to switch to the third location if you're obviously going to lose, but don't spread yourself too thin. Work your cards where it's going to count.

2

Use the locations

■ Every location has an impact on how the game plays out, so read the text on each as it's revealed to make sure you understand its effects. It might change when you can play a card there or the type of card you can play, or there might be something that makes particular cards more or less useful in that spot. Understanding these things can help you build your strategy and plan ahead.

On Reveal: Afflict all enemy cards here with -1 Power.

On Reveal: Activate the On Reveal abilities of your other cards at this location.

Balance your deck

■ Deck building is an art in *Marvel Snap*, but there's no point filling up a deck with heroes and villains that will cost you five or six energy to play—you'll end up being unable to afford to play anything while you're in the early rounds. Instead, keep a balance between high- and low-cost cards, and remember that you can always play several low-cost cards in the final rounds if you need to. Sometimes, it's the best choice!

Build around your big cards

■ Try to work out strategies around the abilities of your big five- and six-point cards. Playing the right cards in the right couple of rounds can really turn a game around. For example, using Odin's power to reactivate on-reveal abilities can give you a lot of extra power in the last round of the game, while Spider-Woman's power-draining ability can even the odds in a close final fight.

■ Some decks will help you win if you play more low-value cards, while others are based around good things happening when you combine a card like Spectrum with a bunch of cards with ongoing effects. Try out different decks for size and find out what works for you!

Upgrade your cards

■ Remember to complete the seasonal and daily missions and claim your rewards. Most importantly, upgrade your cards. Upgrades are only cosmetic, but they increase your collection level, unlocking more cards and more upgrade resources. With more cards, you can open up new strategies, which makes you more unpredictable and harder to beat.

Know when to Snap and when to Retreat

■ Snapping is a real show of confidence, and the best time to do it is when you feel sure that you're going to win. You can even bluff your opponent into a retreat, especially if they can't predict which cards you're going to play and where—or why! On the other hand, if it looks like you're losing, there's no shame in clicking Retreat yourself. You won't lose as many cubes and everybody does it sometimes!

TOP 10 SUPERHERO GAMES

Looking to become a caped crusader or join the ranks of Earth's mightiest heroes? These are the games to do it in.

09 Lego DC Super Villains

■ The *Lego Batman* games have always been a ton of fun, but *Lego DC Super Villains* turns the tables by making the bad guys the heroes. With the Justice League exiled to another universe and replaced by the shifty-looking Justice Syndicate, it's up to the Joker, Harley Quinn, Catwoman, and a bunch of criminal masterminds and misfits to hunt down the truth and save Earth. The puzzles and fighting are right up there with the Lego series' best. On top of collecting classic DC heroes and villains, you can also make and upgrade your own!

AVAILABLE ON: Xbox Series S/X, PS5, Xbox One, PS4, Nintendo Switch, PC

10 Marvel Ultimate Alliance 3: The Black Order

■ The first two *Ultimate Alliance* games are stone-cold superhero classics, so it's a shame they're not available on console or PC today. Luckily, you can get your hands on *The Black Order*, released ten years after the second game as an exclusive for Nintendo Switch. Like the previous games, it's a fast-paced action RPG, where you can put your ultimate super team together from the X-Men, the Guardians of the Galaxy, the Avengers, Spider-Man, and more. You'll need all the super muscle you can get, as you're up against Thanos and his deadly Warmasters on a quest for the Infinity Stones.

AVAILABLE ON: Nintendo Switch

08 Ultimate Marvel vs. Capcom 3

■ Capcom's mighty crossover fighting series hit its peak with this bombastic brawler, pitting all your favorite Marvel stars against Capcom's toughest warriors. If you want to see Doctor Doom, Hulk, Wolverine, and Doctor Strange take on *Devil May Cry*'s Dante and *Street Fighter*'s Chun-Li, this is the game for you, and it even has a cool story to explain it all. With over forty-eight characters and incredible X-Factor abilities, there's something for everyone, while the comic-book graphics still hold up today.

AVAILABLE ON: Xbox One, PS4

06 Marvel's Guardians of the Galaxy

■ Star-Lord and his team look closer to their comic versions than the Marvel movies' stars, but get past that and *Marvel's Guardians of the Galaxy* is an all-time great sci-fi superhero game. It's a chance to explore some of the stranger corners of the Marvel universe, as the Guardians' schemes to get rich quick go so very wrong, putting them on a collision course with a mysterious cult. It's a game stuffed full with awesome adventuring and storming combat, where you have to harness each Guardian's abilities if you want to survive. It's laugh-out-loud funny, too.

AVAILABLE ON: Xbox Series S/X, PS5, Xbox One, PS4, PC

07 The Wonderful 101 Remastered

■ You won't recognize the heroes, but what other game lets you head an army of one hundred costumed champs? When aliens invade Earth, Wonder-Red and his super-buds fight, rescuing people who can turn hero and join the crew. The bigger the gang, the more powerful it is, with your heroes able to "unite morph" into a fist or a skyscraper-size sword to give the invaders the smackdown they deserve. Weird but— like the title says— wonderful.

AVAILABLE ON: Nintendo Switch, PC

04 Injustice 2

■ It has its own dark and gritty take on the DC Comics universe, but *Injustice 2* just about beats *Marvel vs. Capcom 3* to the punch as the best superpowered beat-'em-up ever. It offers up dozens of DC heroes and villains to battle with, giving you everyone from Batman and Superman to Blue Beetle, Starfire, and Gorilla Grodd. All their awesome powers are yours to wield in combat, and you can even customize your stars with new looks, weapons, and gadgets. Forget *Batman vs.*

AVAILABLE ON: Xbox Series S/X, PS5, Xbox One, PS4, PC

Superman: Dawn of Justice—this is the comic-book clash you've been waiting for!

05 Fortnite

■ What's that? *Fortnite*'s not a superhero game? Well, what other massive online game has thrown in so many favorite Marvel and DC heroes? From Batman, Catwoman, and the Joker to Iron Man, Wolverine, and Deadpool, it's not only given us the costumes but unique abilities and weapons, and even themed map locations where you could grab the latest Stark Industries gear or an Armored Batman suit. This crossover even spawned two comic-book miniseries, *Batman/Fortnite: Foundation* and *Batman/Fortnite: Zero Point*.

AVAILABLE ON: Xbox Series S/X, PS5, Xbox One, PS4, Nintendo Switch, PC

03 Lego Marvel Super Heroes 2

■ All the *Lego Marvel* games have been good, but *Lego Marvel Super Heroes 2* is a total epic, pitting all of Marvel's mightiest heroes against the fiendish Kang the Conqueror, as he and his alien invaders conquer first New York City, then Earth. Amazingly, it betters the first *Lego Marvel Super Heroes* for iconic Marvel locations, then packs in even more heroes and villains, including some of the weirdest and most obscure stars. Smart, funny, and incredibly absorbing, it's a must for Marvel fans.

AVAILABLE ON: Xbox Series S/X, PS5, Xbox One, PS4, Nintendo Switch, PC

02 Batman: Arkham City

■ It's a bit too gritty and edgy for younger players, but the *Arkham* games were the first to properly do justice to the Dark Knight and his world. The second game is the best of the bunch, letting the Batman roam free across a chunk of Gotham transformed into a maximum-security prison, its courthouses, museums, and factories becoming hideouts for old Bat's most terrifying foes. From the detective sections to the combat, it's the game that makes you feel like Batman.

AVAILABLE ON: Xbox Series S/X, PS5, Xbox One, PS4, PC

FAST FACT

Spider-Man and Batman are the most popular superheroes in gaming. Each has starred or been featured in over fifty games. Spider-Man got there first, though, making his debut on the Atari VCS in 1982's *Spider-Man*. Batman didn't get his first game until 1986!

01 Marvel's Spider-Man

■ There can be only one game in the frame for the number-one spot—unless you count its expansion starring Miles Morales. *Marvel's Spider-Man* is the perfect superhero game, putting you right in the shoes of your friendly neighborhood wall crawler, in a story that brings in a bunch of classic Spidey villains, not to mention classic Spidey themes. Most of all, it captures the feel of web-slinging around the city, with an amazing acrobatic move set and some brilliant combat moves. Play this, then *Marvel's Spider-Man: Miles Morales* and you'll see what a real superhero game is made of.

AVAILABLE ON: PS5, PC

Capture

141

THE MIGHTY WORLD OF MINECRAFT

Minecraft still has all the magic!

It's now fourteen years since coder Markus "Notch" Persson first released his experimental game, *Minecraft*. In that time the game has evolved massively, spawning endless merchandise, countless imitations, and a range of official spin-offs. Yet it's never lost the core of exploration, creativity, and wonder that made it such a hit. There are good reasons why millions of gamers still play it every day, and why it still gets so much love!

MAKING MINECRAFT

■ Notch developed *Minecraft* in 2009, in part using code and resources he'd worked on for two other unreleased games, *Rubylands* dungeon game and *Zombie Town*. Working with an experimental 3D graphics engine that produced distinctive, blocky 3D "pixels," Notch took inspiration from a building game he'd been playing, *Infiniminer*, and created a game he code-named *Cave Game*. *Cave Game* then quickly morphed into the *Minecraft* we all know today.

■ *Minecraft* was first released in May 2009 on a forum for indie game developers. It built up some buzz in the indie game community, and by the time Notch released the Alpha version in 2010, other gamers were starting to take interest. New items, blocks, mobs, and game mechanics were added, along with Survival mode. *Minecraft* didn't look like anything else, and gamers found its new build and survive mechanics incredibly absorbing. What's more, new tools and blocks enabled players to get creative in a way they had never been before, transforming *Minecraft* into a kind of digital Lego.

■ Notch left his day job behind and worked on *Minecraft* full-time with his Swedish company, Mojang. When the Beta version was released in early 2011, Mojang sold a million digital downloads in the first month. By November, it had over 16 million players. From there *Minecraft* has only grown bigger and better, releasing on everything from consoles to smartphones, and becoming the biggest-selling video game of all time!

RTX
ON

MINECRAFT'S FUTURE

■ In 2014, Microsoft bought Mojang. While many feared this would lead to *Minecraft* becoming an Xbox and PC exclusive, Microsoft has actually pushed *Minecraft* to more computers and devices than ever, while expanding the universe through expansion packs that tie in with the worlds of DC Comics, SpongeBob SquarePants, and Star Wars. We've had spin-offs that take *Minecraft* into new gaming genres, with adventure games, dungeon crawlers, and strategy games.

■ Most of all, *Minecraft* keeps on moving forward, thanks to a huge creative community that continues to develop new worlds, modes, story lines, and modifications, and Mojang's own efforts to add new tools and features for fans to play with. Deep underground realms and mangrove swamps have opened up new biomes for exploration, while new mobs leave players facing perils that they've never faced before. As *Minecraft* wins over a new generation of gamers, one thing is for sure: it still has what it takes to be the world's most popular game.

SEE THE LIGHT!

■ If you want to see what the *Minecraft* of the future looks like, check out the special RTX version on PC. This uses the ray-tracing capabilities of today's PC graphics processors to simulate how light from the game's sun and other light sources would reflect off every surface, creating some of the most realistic lighting, shading, and reflection effects you can see in any video game. It transforms the way *Minecraft* looks. Lights and torches create pools of colored lights while objects, mobs, and scenery have natural-looking shadows. *Minecraft*'s blocky looks have always been a big part of its charm, but with ray tracing, the game looks amazing!

MINECRAFT DUNGEONS

■ *Minecraft Dungeons* didn't make a massive impact at its 2020 launch, but since then it's become a brilliant game in its own right. It's basically *Minecraft* meets the classic dungeon crawler *Diablo*, but with fantastic four-player co-op and an evolving story line, it's actually even better than that sounds!

PASS THE TESTS
GENTLE BREEZE

■ You can spend months battling your way through the game's monster-haunted ruins and perilous underground lairs, fighting hordes of familiar bad guys along with some new sword and sorcery foes. Collecting and upgrading enchanted weapons and armor never gets old, and Mojang has done a great job of keeping things interesting with seasonal updates and add-on packs. It's secretly one of the best co-op games out there, and you don't need an Xbox to play it. It's also available on PS4, PC, and Nintendo Switch!

FAST FACT

Thanks to its accessibility and the ability to code within the game, *Minecraft* has been used in schools around the world. Teachers have used it to teach everything from programming to city planning, environmental studies, math, and physics. Microsoft even makes a free Education Edition version of the game.

MINECRAFT LEGENDS

■ *Minecraft Legends* does for the strategy game what *Minecraft Dungeons* did for the dungeon crawler. It takes all your favorite Minecraft NPCs and mobs and makes them troops and support units in a mighty *Minecraft* army!

■ The Overworld is under threat once more, from a fiendish Piglin army. Using the power of the Nether, they're working to corrupt the world, its animals, and its people to use for their own evil ends. At first, only a single square-jawed hero stands in their way, but it won't take you long to unite the people of the Overworld and send the Piglin forces packing.

MINECRAFT LEGENDS

THE TOP EXPANSION PACKS

■ *Minecraft* is great for tie-ins and mash-ups, as anyone who's seen the Switch version's Mario-themed worlds will know. With *Minecraft*-ready heroes, villains, worlds, and ready-made adventures, these DLC packs give you a new way to enjoy your favorite stars in your favorite game!

LIGHTYEAR DLC

■ Inspired by the 2022 movie, the *Lightyear DLC* puts you straight into the Space Ranger's origin story, as Buzz battles to survive the alien planet he's crash-landed onto.

As well as Buzz's escape adventure, this expansion includes a bunch of new costumes to try and space vehicles to fly, along with a cool *Lightyear*-themed character creator.

BATMAN DLC

■ Having conquered the world of Lego in games and movies, the Dark Knight is a natural for *Minecraft*. This DLC gives you a puzzle-packed adventure in a *Minecraft* Gotham City, complete with Wayne Manor, the Batcave, and Batman's most famous enemies and allies. Our blocky caped crusader also comes with some awesome gadgets, including the batarang, the batclaw grappling hook, and his mighty fighting gauntlets.

SPONGEBOB SQUAREPANTS DLC

■ Fancy a trip to Bikini Bottom? The *SpongeBob SquarePants DLC* will take you there, Minecraft style. You can explore familiar locations like the blocky Reef Cinema and SpongeBob's Pineapple House, and there's a whole adventure with tons of cool stuff to collect. Plus, you get SpongeBob and his friends to play with.

HIGH-SPEED STRATEGY

■ The action mixes classic real-time strategy with a touch of Nintendo favorite *Pikmin* as you recruit your troops, upgrade their gear, and lead them into action.

ENEMIES TO ALLIES

■ Your mission is to unite the Overworld—and that includes its monsters. Even old foes like the Creepers, Zombies, and Skeletons can join your side!

FROM JOYSTICKS TO

See how the console controller has evolved

DUALSENSE

G ames have changed a lot in the past forty-five years, and controllers have had to change with them. From D-pads to analog sticks, the Rumble Pak to the Impulse Trigger, they keep making games deeper, more fun, and more immersive.

1985

NINTENDO NES CONTROLLER

■ Nintendo changed the gaming world with the Nintendo Entertainment System, and its controller was just as revolutionary. It ditched the joystick for the four-way D-pad that was used in Nintendo's Game & Watch handheld games, then added a second button. Nintendo's pad was tough and perfect for the new *Mario Bros.* platform games.

1978

ATARI CX40 JOYSTICK

■ The first console games kept things simple—you moved, you blasted, you jumped. All they needed was the most basic controller: a sturdy joystick with a single button. Originally bundled with the Atari 2600 or VCS, this joystick and its imitators became the standard controller for gaming for nearly ten years, working across both Atari's consoles and the early home computers.

SEGA GENESIS CONTROLLER

1989

■ Sega's Genesis was a more sophisticated console, aimed at an older audience, and its controller was made to match. Its chunky shape was easier to grip, and with three buttons and an eight-way D-pad, it was ready for anything, from shoot-'em-ups and epic RPGs, to the ongoing adventures of *Sonic the Hedgehog*. Later versions added an extra three buttons for mastering fighting games.

1991

SUPER NES CONTROLLER

■ With its two-tone gray design and buttons and rounded shape, the Super NES controller didn't have the cool looks of the Sega Genesis pad. What it did have, though, was two shoulder buttons, which gamers used for cool new tricks like sliding karts around corners or pulling off your strongest punches and kicks. Games like *Street Fighter II*, *Starfox*, and *Mario Kart* used these to full effect!

SONY PLAYSTATION CONTROLLER

■ Sony's PlayStation Controller was a radical design, with the twin-grip shape Sony was still using twenty-five years later, with the D-pad on the left and the action buttons on the right—already showing those iconic PlayStation shapes. Sony also took Nintendo's shoulder buttons and ran with them, putting four right where your fingers could quickly find them.

1994

1996

N64 CONTROLLER

■ Trust Nintendo to come up with something as wacky as this. The "trident" style was soon abandoned, but the analog stick was here to stay, giving players the full 3D control they needed to master games like *Goldeneye* and *Super Mario 64*. The optional Rumble Pak also added cool vibration effects to your games for the first time, jolting your joypad when you fired off a shot in your favorite shooters or took a hit in *Killer Instinct 64*!

1997

SONY DUALSHOCK
■ With 3D games on the rise, every console needed an analog stick, but Sony went one better and gave us two! With the DualShock on the original PSX, you could finally move, aim, and shoot at the same time, or use one stick to steer your car in *Gran Turismo* and the other to put your foot down on the gas! The DualShock also had built-in rumble plus larger L2 and R2 buttons that were easier to squeeze.

FAST FACT

The first controller with a thumbstick didn't come from Sega or Nintendo, but from arcade fighting game and shoot-'em-up specialist SNK. Its Neo-Geo CD console (1994) shipped with a controller that swapped the D-pad for a shrunk-down stick with an imprint for your thumb. It was still a digital stick, however, tracking the direction but not the distance or the speed of movement.

1998

2002

2006

SEGA DREAMCAST CONTROLLER
■ Sega's Dreamcast controller is now seen as a classic, even if Sega hadn't seen the point of having two analog sticks! It was the first controller with analog triggers, giving you smooth brake and gas pedals in *Sega GT*, *Crazy Taxi*, and the awesome *Metropolis Street Racer*. And the hole? Here you could insert Sega's weird VMUs, which provided both storage for your saved games and a basic black-and-white handheld console for playing weird spin-off games. Nuts!

MICROSOFT XBOX CONTROLLER S
■ Microsoft's original Xbox controller was a massive round monster, which some gamers nicknamed "The Duke" and others compared to a dinner plate. Microsoft turned things around when it launched the Xbox in Japan with the new Controller S. It was smaller, with a more elegant design, but still had the four colored action buttons and central X. The Controller S evolved into the classic Xbox 360 design.

NINTENDO WII REMOTE
■ Nintendo's Wii was all about the motion controls and the ingenious Wii Remote. Suddenly, you could play tennis by serving, smashing, and lobbing with your slim remote, or blast your foes by pointing at the screen and pulling the trigger. And when you needed an analog stick? Just plug in the Nunchuk accessory and you were primed for adventure. You can still see the Wii Remote's DNA in the Switch's Joy-Cons!

SONY SIXAXIS

■ Sony wasn't missing out on this motion control stuff, so the PlayStation 3 launched with a reworked DualShock 2 controller with built-in sensors for motion control. While these worked great for driving and flying, they couldn't do all the clever stuff the Wii Remote could do. Worse, the Sixaxis lost the rumble features of the DualShock and DualShock 2, which only returned with the upgraded DualShock 3.

2006

2013

SONY DUALSHOCK 4

■ Sony didn't throw the classic DualShock design out the window for the PS4, but it made some interesting additions. The big one was the new touchpad, which you could use for simple gestures or to move a cursor on the screen. Meanwhile, a glowing bar at the rear could give you in-game info on your status, or could be used with the PlayStation camera for basic motion controls. Sony also made this the first wireless controller with a built-in standard headphone socket. And who could resist those special edition colors?

XBOX ELITE CONTROLLER

■ Microsoft went to town with its Xbox One super-controller, with swappable thumb sticks and D-pads, including new metal options, customizable paddles on the rear, and triggers you could tune for sensitivity. And it still had all the goodies of the original Xbox One controller, including its awesome vibrating Impulse Triggers. E-sports champs went big for the Elite, creating a new trend for premium controllers.

2015

2020

SONY DUALSENSE

■ Sony's PlayStation 5 DualSense controller is the first to really shift away from the DualShock style. It still has the same set of features as the DualShock 4, but also a couple of cool new tricks. Its adaptive triggers use tiny motors to simulate rumble and resistance, giving you guns with a stiffer trigger, or a gas pedal that pushes back as you press it down. Beyond that, you have the new haptic feedback features, with more detailed rumble effects that take you right into the game. Now that's what we call immersion!

TOP 10 INDIE GAMES

Looking for the weirdest, most imaginative games? Today's indie hits prove you don't need a big budget to build something brilliant.

10 Curse of the Sea Rats

■ Transformed into rats by a pirate witch, four plucky prisoners of the British Empire have just one hope of getting their human bodies back: to find her and force her to remove her curse, even if that means battling every deadly boss along the way. This awesome "metroidvania" style adventure has gorgeous hand-drawn cartoon graphics, swashbuckling swordplay, and a lovable cast of rodent rogues to meet and duel.

AVAILABLE ON:
Nintendo Switch, PS5, PS4, Xbox One, Xbox Series S/X, PC

09 The Plucky Squire

■ An adventure that starts out in the pages of a picture book turns into something truly extraordinary, as our plucky squire hero ventures outside his 2D paper world to explore the 3D world beyond. It's a great concept brought to life with some fantastically imaginative graphics, as the tale takes our hero out of the book, to the bedroom, and beyond.

AVAILABLE ON:
Nintendo Switch, PS5, Xbox Series S/X, PC

08 Sea of Stars

■ The team that brought us *The Messenger* is back, but instead of another ninja platformer, this time we've got a new spin on the classic 16-bit Japanese RPGs. In it, your team of feisty Soulstice Knights is called to arms against an evil alchemist and his diabolical creations. Luckily, while he can reanimate the dead, you can command the powers of sun and moon. This is an epic full of tactical combat, heart, and magic, complete with awesome retro pixel graphics.

AVAILABLE ON:
Nintendo Switch, PS5, PS4, PC

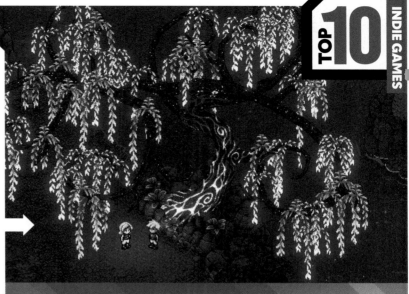

07 Bomb Rush Cyberfunk

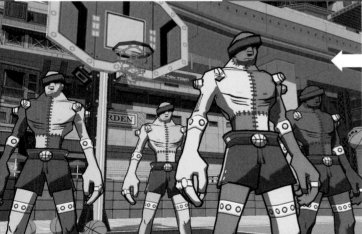

■ Back in the day, Sega made a game called *Jet Set Radio*, where cartoon skaters took on an evil corporation in a cartoon city of the future. *Bomb Rush Cyberfunk* is a tribute and a spiritual sequel, where your skaters and freestyle BMXers need to trick, grind, and boost their way to the farthest, highest reaches of the city, laying down graffiti to prove they rule the roost. It's just too funky to be missed.

AVAILABLE ON: Nintendo Switch, PC

06 Paleo Pines

■ What could be better than another great life sim in the style of *Stardew Valley* or *Animal Crossing*? How about one with dinosaurs? In *Paleo Pines*, you and your pioneer friends have to share your island home with dinos. Don't worry— they're friendly, and they'll even let you ride them or help you out on your growing ranch! You've got huge areas to explore and lots of dino-friends to make, or just chill out and enjoy the cool Jurassic vibes.

AVAILABLE ON: PC

05 Little Bear Chef

■ Life's tough when you're trying to make a name as a master chef—and even tougher when you're a tiny little bear trying to work in a human-size kitchen. Just getting your ingredients together is a challenge, and that's before you try to chop them with a knife bigger than you are. This brilliant 3D platform/cooking/puzzle game has a lot of fun with its half-pint hero, and you'd better believe that this bear chef is destined for great things!

AVAILABLE ON: Nintendo Switch, PC

04 Sports Story

■ The sequel to *Golf Story* is another weird retro RPG with a sporty twist, only this time you're raiding dungeons and abandoned ruins for treasure while tackling tennis, soccer, BMX, fishing, volleyball, and more. And when you're not in a competition or out on a quest, why not chill out with a trip to the mall? We loved the original for its mix of adventure and silly sports action, but *Sports Story* takes it up to a whole new level!

AVAILABLE ON: Nintendo Switch

03 Oni: Road to Be the Mightiest Oni

■ On a small island in the middle of an ocean, a grumpy little demon and his ghostly friend take on the island's other monsters to prove their worthiness to fight the biggest demon of them all. Imagine Nintendo doing a game like *Dark Souls*, but with lovable cartoon graphics, a hero you can't help rooting for, and a wicked sense of humor. *Oni: Road to Be the Mightiest Oni* is the nearest thing.

AVAILABLE ON: Nintendo Switch, PS5, PS4, PC

02 Blanc

■ *Blanc* looks like hand-drawn pen-and-paper sketches brought to life, partly because its scenes and characters were all sketched out that way and scanned in through a computer before being turned into 3D graphics. And if the style doesn't get you, this tale of a lost fawn and wolf cub working together to battle the freezing cold and overcome obstacles on their way back home certainly will. Designed for two players, it's one of the year's best co-op games.

AVAILABLE ON:
Nintendo Switch, PC

01 Cassette Beasts

■ Do you know someone annoying who keeps on saying that the old 2D *Pokémon* games are the best? *Cassette Beasts* leaves you thinking they might have a point. This is a triple-whammy of retro nostalgia, combining pixel graphics with classic monster collecting and battles, then following up with a cool 1980s vibe. It's even got its own ingenious twist. By combining any two monsters, you can create your own unique hybrid forms!

AVAILABLE ON: Nintendo Switch, Xbox One, Xbox Series S/X, PC

FAST FACT

It's no accident if *Sea of Stars* sounds like a classic nineties JRPG. Its music was composed by Yasunori Mitsuda, who composed the music for the legendary *Chrono Trigger* and *Chrono Cross* games!

HARVESTELLA

FARM, FISH, AND FIGHT YOUR WAY TO A BRIGHTER FUTURE

Go to the deepest point in High...Cave Spring Ze...enth Saturday 10:42 Dem

A deadly magic plague threatens the fantasy world of *Harvestella*. Every time the Quietus hits, a cursed dust drops from the skies, withering the crops in the fields and sickening anyone caught outdoors. Together, your mysterious hero, a girl from the future, and a growing gang of misfits have to stop it and safeguard the four giant crystals that keep the seasons changing. But in *Harvestella* that's not all. You've got a farm to rebuild, your own crops to grow, animals to take care of, and five towns full of people to help. Better get busy!

QUICK TIPS

FIX IT UP
■ *Harvestella*'s wilderness areas and dungeons are full of broken ladders and bridges. Repair them, as they'll give you shortcuts to avoid danger and reach your quest objectives faster.

FREE FOOD
■ Early on, you won't have a kitchen to cook your own meals, but the leaves and berries you find in the dungeons can be eaten raw, and you'll still get a health boost when you eat them.

TAKE IT EASY
■ Though it seems like there's a rush to save the world, don't sweat it. It's worth taking your time early on to grow and sell crops and get your first renovations done.

FIGHT EVIL, WORK THE LAND

■ There's more to *Harvestella* than exploring dungeons and battling monsters. Growing and selling crops is the best way to make money, and you'll need the cash to upgrade your tools and weapons, and turn your rickety farmhouse into a hero HQ.

TOIL ON THE SOIL

■ Plow your fields, sow your seeds, and give the growing plants water, and you'll soon be rewarded with wheat and veg. Pop your harvest in the blue delivery box and it's sold automatically.

LEARN ON THE JOB

■ You need skills to battle monsters, and that means mastering a system of jobs. *Harvestella* has twelve jobs you can switch between at will, and each brings new fighting skills to learn and use.

GET FISHING

■ Fishing is another good way to get some cash. You can sell what you catch or cook it up to make a tempting meal. You can also learn how to fish by buying the book from the general store.

POWERFUL FRIENDS, POWERFUL ENEMIES

■ Follow the main story quests and you'll make awesome new friends with their own unique abilities. Watch out, though: you'll also make enemies who need to be defeated!

FAST FACT

Harvestella's developer, Live Wire, has a thing about cursed weather. Its previous game, *Ender Lilies: Quietus of the Knights*, was all about a rain that turned people into undead monsters!

LIKE THIS? TRY THIS:

RUNE FACTORY 5

■ The original farming and dungeon crawling RPG is still going strong. While *Rune Factory 5* doesn't have *Harvestella*'s epic story, it makes up for it with cartoon graphics and easygoing charm.

STORY OF SEASONS: IT'S A WONDERFUL LIFE

TAKE A BREAK FROM THE REAL WORLD WITH A LIFE SIM CLASSIC

Long before *Stardew Valley*, *Animal Crossing*, and the rest, the *Story of Seasons* series was pioneering the video game sim of a rugged outdoor life. Many fans believe 2003's *A Wonderful Life* is the peak of the series, so it's great to see this classic return in a full-on remake. Want to farm without the hard work and smelly stuff? Make friends in town, meet someone special, and maybe start a family? This is the game for you!

Your farm might not look like much to begin with—just a few fields, a dog, and a cow—but with a bit of grit you can turn it into something special, and start your wonderful life.

QUICK TIPS

HAGGLE

■ If you're selling stuff to Van, try haggling. Refuse his first offer and he'll usually offer more on the second try. Sometimes you can even get lucky and get more from a third offer.

SAVE YOUR LEGS

■ Once you get a horse, ride it everywhere. You'll save time and stamina, making it easier to get more done during a working day.

GONE FISHIN'

■ Fishing is a great way to make cash early on. Buy the fishing pole and find spots on the river or by waterfalls where you're sure to catch something big—if you're patient!

LIVING YOUR BEST LIFE

■ Making the most of *A Wonderful Life* is all about balancing hard work with fun. Make sure you stay on top of your chores, but take some time out to explore the world around you, make friends, and even find some magic in the countryside.

GET TO WORK

■ Prepare your land, plant your crops, and give them plenty of water. You'll soon have stuff to eat and sell. Remember to buy new seeds before each new season!

LOOK AFTER THE LIVESTOCK

■ Cows, sheep, ducks, and chickens all need your attention, whether that's milking your cows, feeding the chickens, or keeping your sheep well-brushed. Most of all, give them lots of love.

PARTNER UP AND RAISE SOME KIDS

■ Some friendships can turn into something more—and before you know it, you'll be starting a family. Will you raise your own little farmer to take over from their mom and dad?

HANG OUT WITH THE LOCALS

■ Rural life still gives you plenty of opportunities to meet and make friends with the neighbors and everyone in town. Be friendly and give the odd thoughtful gift to build your relationships.

FAST FACT

In the remake you can play as a boy or as a girl, but in the original *A Wonderful Life* you had to be a boy. If you wanted to play as a girl, you had to wait over six months for a second game, *Another Wonderful Life*—or, in Japan, *A Wonderful Life for Girls*!

LIKE THIS? TRY THIS:

STARDEW VALLEY

■ The massive indie hit was inspired by the classic *Story of Seasons* games but has some great ideas of its own. If you're looking for a slightly more complex life sim, they don't get much better.

DISNEY DREAMLIGHT VALLEY

How to get ahead in Disney's magical life sim

Most of us had *Disney Dreamlight Valley* pegged as *Animal Crossing* with a Disney and Pixar cast, but there's more to it than that. While you can spend time building and decorating your village, it's really more about recovering a world that's been forgotten, and finding and befriending your favorite Disney stars and villains. There's a lot to discover, plenty to craft, and even more stuff to collect! If you're finding some of that hard going, we've got hints and tips to help.

1

It's all mine!

■ Early on, you'll be short of cash. You can get hold of some by pulling up Night Thorns, and more by catching and selling fish, but the easiest way to get a lot of money quickly is by smashing up the rocks with sparkling gemstones and selling all the gems you find. These regenerate daily, and even the first Plaza and Peaceful Meadow areas have garnets and peridots to mine!

Farm and forage

2

■ Whatever else you're doing, keep collecting useful stuff. Harvest fruit and vegetables when you see them, grab some hardwood or softwood, and pause to fish when you get a chance. You can always take it home and store it in a chest, and it will make your life a lot easier when you're asked to find materials by one of your Dreamlight Valley friends. Remember to plant any seeds you find and water them, too. It's free food!

DREAMLIGHT BUDDIES:
Moana

■ Moana needs help fixing her canoe and finding a place to live. She's also missing a much-loved pet. Help her out and you'll have a friend for life! Her favorite foods tend to have a fishy flavor, although she's also keen on apple pie.

FAST FACT

Disney Dreamlight Valley features many of the stars that voiced the original movies, including Tim Allen as Buzz Lightyear, Pat Carroll as Ursula, Jodi Benson as Ariel, and Chloe Auli'i Cravalho as Moana.

3

Upgrade your backpack

■ The only problem with foraging is that you'll fill your backpack fast. That's why you should upgrade it as soon as you can. It's an expensive upgrade—5,000 Star Coins—but having double the slots to fill will save you a lot of time and hassle, even early on.

4

Build more storage

■ You'll also need space to store all that stuff until you need it. You can upgrade your house and upgrade your first chest, but it's going to cost you big time! In the early stages, it's more realistic to gather softwood and rocks and just build another chest. You can put them inside or around your house, and with a couple you'll have plenty of space for all your rocks, wood, food, and more!

DREAMLIGHT BADDIES:
Scar

■ Even bad guys can be helped in Dreamlight Valley. Scar wants to put the Sunlit Plateau area back on the map, but you'll need some nice food to stop this regal snob from munching on the other villagers. Luckily, he's a huge fan of fish dishes and shiny jewels.

5

Catch of the day

■ Want to catch the biggest fish? Look for ponds or stretches of river with blue or red bubble rings. Try to cast your line inside the ring and prepare for a challenge—you might have to get the timing right three or four times! It's worth it, though, as you could land a whopper!

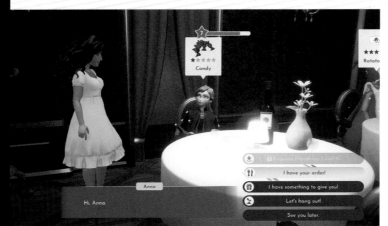

Fancy eating

■ Feeding your valley friends their favorite foods is an easy way to boost their friendship, but you can get an even bigger boost if you do it while they're sitting in Remy's restaurant. You'll need to finish Remy's first questline and re-open Chez Remy, but once that's done, you can take your friends' restaurant orders and cook them up in the restaurant kitchen. Hand over the requested dish and you'll get a whopping Friendship upgrade, depending on the star grade of the food.

Do your duties

7

■ Dreamlight is the most important resource in the game, and the best way to get it is to do your Dreamlight Duties. You can check what these are from the Dreamlight tab in the main menu, but you'll get a lot of them completed just through mining, collecting, selling, and even taking the odd photo or selfie. Remember to head back to the menu to collect your Dreamlight bounty!

Charm the wildlife

8

■ See those adorable squirrels and rabbits? They're not just for show. Find out how to approach each type of critter, then give it its favorite food, and you can make friends with them. Keep at it and they can become an animal companion, complete with cool outfits if you can earn or buy the right items. It's not just the friendly animals, either. How about a raven or crocodile companion?

DREAMLIGHT BUDDIES:
Ariel

■ The star of *The Little Mermaid* is stranded on a distant beach. You'll need your own raft just to reach her, then you need to help her find her own way home! She'll only turn up in rivers, ponds, and the sea, but it's still worth boosting your Friendship with Gazpacho, Black Passion Lilies, and Fruit Sorbets.

RECIPES

Select a Recipe

	Bell Pepper Puffs	★★★☆☆
	Crackers	★☆☆☆☆
	Grilled Vegetables	★☆☆☆☆
	Fish Soup	★★★☆☆
	Fruit Salad	★☆☆☆☆

Start Cooking 1

B Close / Remove Ingredients

9 Restore your energy

■ Running out of energy can hold you back, but there are two ways to restore it. The first is just to go home. You don't need to sleep—just step through the door and the bar will refill. Away from home, though, your best bet is a tasty meal. Cook up a bunch of easy meals before you head off on an adventure and then you can top up whenever you need to.

DREAMLIGHT BADDIES: Mother Gothel

■ She's nobody's idea of a great mom, but that doesn't mean you can't make friends with *Tangled*'s villain. You'll need to release her from a cursed tree and do some work with Ursula, the sea witch, too! Mother Gothel is often partial to Eggplant, Pumpkin Soup, and tasty Kappa Maki sushi!

10 Hang out with your friends

■ Mickey, Donald, Goofy, and your other pals can do more than give you missions and eat your snacks. Ask them to hang out with you and they'll follow you around, and by assigning them a role, you can get useful perks that will help you when you're gardening, mining, digging, foraging, or fishing. Best of all, when they hang out with you, their Friendship level increases, so you can speed up your progress just by spending time with your best buds!

Pikmin 4

What is a Pikmin and what can they do? Find out more in our beginner's guide.

■ It's been twenty-two years since the brave Captain Olimar first crash-landed on an alien planet and discovered a new form of life! Called Pikmin, these cute little critters grew from seeds to become a stranded astronaut's best friend. Since then we've learned much about the Pikmin and their strange life cycle—and it's not too late for you to learn all about them before you play *Pikmin 4*.

Meet the Pikmin

■ Think of the Pikmin as your eager troops and workers—look after them, and they'll look after you. They come in different types and colors, with each displaying different strengths and weaknesses. Red Pikmin are fire-resistant and fierce in combat, while Yellow Pikmin are lighter and can be thrown much farther. Purple Pikmin are slow but strong, while Ice Pikmin have special freezing powers. You'll have to find out for yourself what other Pikmin can do!

FAST FACT

As Pikmin age, the stem on their head changes to reveal their growing skills and status. They start off with a single leaf, which transforms into a bud, which eventually turns into a flower. Drinking nectar is the surest way for a Pikmin to develop to the next stage.

Breeding Pikmin

■ Pikmin can be found wandering around distant alien planets, but they reproduce through their own eccentric process. If food—including insect meat and vegetables—is dragged back to a strange Pikmin structure called an "onion," then it will be digested and transformed into a scattering of Pikmin seedlings. Left to mature, these can be pulled up to reveal young Pikmin, ready at once to join your crew.

Pikmin power!

■ Pikmin can carry objects many times their weight, working together to share their strength. The more Pikmin you throw at an obstacle, the faster they'll remove it; the more you ask to shift an object, the faster they'll get it where it needs to go. They can also smash through barriers, collect food, and save any Pikmin buddies that have wandered into trouble.

Pikmin's best friend

■ This two-legged, dog-like creature has only recently been spotted, but seems happy and well equipped to aid its Pikmin friends and their explorer leaders. It can carry both around on its back to cross challenging territory, and also makes a useful ally when you have to charge into battle or escape from a fight you're losing.

Tiny troopers

■ Pikmin have to face attacks from insect and mollusk predators, who love nothing more than to gobble 'em up! Luckily, the courageous Pikmin can fight together to bring down the biggest insects, thinking nothing of sacrificing their own lives to save their friends. Keep throwing them at their foes and they're sure to triumph— especially if you use their specific powers! And the remains can be digested to create more Pikmin!

DRAGON QUEST TREASURES

THIS TIME IT'S ALL ABOUT THE LOOT!

Let's go!

Get ready for a different kind of *Dragon Quest*—one where you make friends with the monsters, and your only goal is to fill your base with a massive pile of treasure! You might recognize our heroes, Erik and Mia, from their adventures in *Dragon Quest XI*, but in this peculiar prequel they're exploring the world of Draconia, and starting up their own gang on the trail of loot. Before you can dig up chests brimming with gold, you're going to need to build a party of warriors. That's where your monster friends come in. Defeat them in battle and they might just ask to join your crew!

QUICK TIPS

© 2022 ARMOR PROJECT/BIRD STUDIO/SQUARE ENIX All Rights Reserved.

TREASURE TRACKERS

■ Your monster friends have awesome treasure-finding senses, so watch out for the treasure chest icon, then use the monster's Treasure Vision to lock down the spot where the loot is hidden.

PLAY SUPPORT

■ Your monsters can handle most of the fighting, so focus on damaging tougher targets with your slingshot and looking after your team with your healing pellets. Don't let them die!

SEND A TEAM

■ Remember that you can send teams of monsters off on treasure-hunting quests of their own. Go hunting with your own crew and your B team will return with even more lovely loot!

BUILDING THE DREAM TEAM

■ Looking to fill up your treasure vault faster? You need to put together a dream team of monsters who can fight your battles and track down the loot.

BUDDY UP

■ It's not enough to beat the monsters. Hit them with a buddy bullet during the fight, then head back to your base and see Miss Cecily. Check out the potential new recruits and see what items they want as a fee to join your crew.

GO TEAM!

■ The monsters will pick their own targets and moves in battle, but that doesn't mean you should just stand and watch. Use your slingshot and daggers to support them, and watch out for the Dragon Attack meter—it's the key to your most powerful moves.

Mogsworth Unbound

PICK YOUR PARTY

■ You can only take three monsters out at once, so pick the monsters who will be most useful in a fight and give you the best chance of finding treasure. Each monster has favorite treasures they can look for, and bigger monsters can also carry more treasure back to base!

UNLEASH THE BEASTS

■ Just hold the R button when the dagger meter is full, then press Y, X, or A to command one of your monsters to use their attack. Or use Erik and Mia's Wild Side attack to give your heroes a boost and their own chance to shine!

FAST FACT

Dragon Quest's creator, Yuji Horii, has worked on every single game in the series, including *Dragon Quest Treasures* and the next major entry, *Dragon Quest XII*. Even when he doesn't direct or produce the game, he still helps the team make the best *Dragon Quest* they can.

LIKE THIS? TRY THIS:

DRAGON QUEST XI S: ECHOES OF AN ELUSIVE AGE

■ Want to see what Erik and Mia do next? *Dragon Quest XI* is one of the best games in the series, especially for *Dragon Quest* noobs. This special edition expands the plot and adds a cool 16-bit graphics mode.

BEYOND FINAL FANTASY:

THE BEST OTHER JAPANESE RPGs

Discover your next favorite RPG

J apan didn't invent the RPG, but it sure worked hard to perfect it. As far back as the 1980s, the teams at Squaresoft, Nihon Falcom, Sega, Capcom, and Enix worked to create amazing fantasy and sci-fi role-playing games that took us to new worlds full of magic and wonder, worlds where monsters lived, fierce battles were fought, and epic story lines stretched out for hour after hour. It says a lot that the series they created still continues today. If you want to go beyond *Final Fantasy*, these are the games and series that you need to try.

THE TALES SERIES (Bandai Namco)

FIRST GAME: *Tales of Phantasia*, 1995
LATEST GAME: *Tales of Arise*, 2021

■ If you're looking for action-packed combat, interesting stories, and a great cast of heroes and villains, it's hard to go wrong with a *Tales* game. The series specializes in sophisticated fantasy worlds full of conflict and intrigue, and for its battles that mix fast-paced swordplay with magical "artes."

TRY: *Tales of Arise* is a great place for new *Tales* players to start, with two amazing worlds and some fascinating characters, along with systems that are easy to get into but have enough depth to stay interesting through the whole game.

THE XENO SAGA (Monolith Soft/Square/ Bandai Namco/Nintendo)

FIRST GAME: *Xenogears*, 1998
LATEST GAME: *Xenoblade Chronicles 3*, 2022

■ The *Xeno* saga has hopped from world to world and console to console, starting off on the PlayStation with *Xenogears* in 1998 and running through the *Xenosaga* series on PlayStation 2, then shifting to the Nintendo Wii, Wii U, and Switch for the *Xenoblade Chronicles* games. They're all linked loosely by their sci-fi meets fantasy settings and complex story lines—and their mix of magic and giant robot mechs.

TRY: You can play the whole *Xenoblade Chronicles* series from beginning to end on the Nintendo Switch, or start with the latest, *Xenoblade Chronicles 3*, and then go back to the HD remake of *Xenoblade Chronicles: Definitive Edition*. Either way, you'll have a blast!

FIRE EMBLEM

(Intelligent Systems/Nintendo)

FIRST GAME: *Fire Emblem: Shadow Dragon and the Blade of Light*, 1990

LATEST GAME: *Fire Emblem Engage*, 2023

■ Nintendo's strategy-RPG series goes all the way back to the original Nintendo Entertainment system, with sequels appearing on every home and handheld console since. From 2005's *Fire Emblem: Path of Radiance*, it's had a mind-blowing mix of magic, turn-by-turn strategy, and emotional stories, where the friendships and choices you make away from the battlefield matter just as much as your tactics on it.

TRY: *Fire Emblem: Three Houses* on the Switch is one of the console's best-loved classics, with a tale of a magical military academy where your hero has signed on as the new teacher. *Fire Emblem: Engage* is made of the same powerful stuff, though, and is also a good way into the series.

STAR OCEAN (Tri-Ace/Square Enix)

FIRST GAME: *Star Ocean*, 1996
LATEST GAME: *Star Ocean: The Divine Force*, 2022

■ *Star Ocean* is the leading sci-fi JRPG, first appearing on the Super NES before making the shift to PlayStation and—these days—PC and Xbox, too. The series has elements of *Star Trek*, *Star Wars*, and classic Japanese sci-fi anime, although you'll see knights, swords, and sorcery as well as starships, laser guns, and droids. With cool characters and strange new worlds to explore, it's a great series for JRPG fans who want to try something different.

TRY: Fans will tell you that *Star Ocean: The Divine Force* is the best *Star Ocean* in years. It helps that it's the only one since 2016, but it's a spectacular entry in the series.

DRAGON QUEST (Enix/Square Enix)

FIRST GAME: *Dragon Quest*, 1986
LATEST GAME: *Dragon Quest XI*, 2018

■ *Dragon Quest* was *Final Fantasy*'s biggest rival in Japan—at least until its maker, Enix, joined *Final Fantasy*'s creator, Squaresoft, to make one awesome RPG powerhouse. Here in the US, it's never quite had the same massive fan base, but the cartoon graphics, lovable heroes, and lighter, more humorous style make it an easy series to love. Where else can you battle smiling blobs of slime, crazed green bats, smirking toadstools, and fiendish feline wizards? No *Dragon Quest* is short of excitement and adventure—and they're always fun!

TRY: *Dragon Quest VIII* is a stone-cold classic, and you can play it on your iPhone or Android phone! *Dragon Quest XI* is another awesome epic, with some of the strongest characters in the series.

KINGDOM HEARTS (Square Enix)

FIRST GAME: *Kingdom Hearts*, 2002
LATEST GAME: *Kingdom Hearts III*, 2019

■ *Kingdom Hearts* is the franchise where *Final Fantasy* meets Disney—and you'll find many of your favorite Pixar characters onboard as well. It's one of the easiest JRPG series to get into, with a more action-packed approach to fighting, and there's no other series where you can join forces with Goofy, Buzz Lightyear, and Jack Sparrow to battle evil.

TRY: Why not tackle the whole saga, starting with *Kingdom Hearts HD 1.5 and 2.5 ReMIX*, before you go on to the fantastic finale, *Kingdom Hearts III*?

YS (Nihon Falcom)

FIRST GAME: *Ys: Ancient Ys Vanished*, 1987

LATEST GAME: *Ys IX: Monstrum Nox*, 2021

■ The *Ys* series has been rolling since the late 1980s. It's huge in Japan and Korea, though it's only in the past few years that it's built much of a fan base in the US. The series is unusual in that every game features the same main hero, Adol Christin, a young swordsman who battles injustice all around the world. Yet Adol is always joined by a crew of warriors, vagabonds, and nobles in tales where the relationships between the characters are as important as their strength and skill.

TRY: *Ys VIII: Lacrimosa of Dana* is the best *Ys* for beginners, with a self-contained story of island castaways that's easier to get into than 2021's *Ys IX: Monstrum Nox*.

MONSTER HUNTER (Capcom)

FIRST GAME: *Monster Hunter*, 2004

LATEST GAME: *Monster Hunter Rise*, 2021

■ Some people question whether it's a real RPG, but Capcom's monster-slaying action RPG series is a global phenomenon! Hunt down giant beasts, collect their hides, claws, bones, and teeth, then turn them into epic-level weapons and armor. There's usually an exciting story line to follow, and the games are designed to be enjoyed online with friends. And who can resist a game where your bodyguard and best buddy is a talking cat?

TRY: *Monster Hunter Rise* on PC, Xbox, and Nintendo Switch is the easiest way into the series, but *Monster Hunter World* on the PS4, PC, and Xbox isn't far behind.

THE ATELIER SERIES

FIRST GAME: *Atelier Marie*, 1997

LATEST GAME: *Atelier Sophie 2: The Alchemist of the Mysterious Dream*, 2022

■ The *Atelier* series is a cult hit that's crossing over into the mainstream. The name actually means "artist's studio" in French, but in the games it's used to describe the young alchemist heroes. Fans love the games because they focus on gathering materials and combining them in magical recipes, as well as on the relationships between the Ateliers and their friends and rivals. If you find *Final Fantasy* and *Tales* too serious, this could be the JRPG for you.

TRY: *Atelier Ryza* is the first game in one of the series' most-loved story lines, and if you get through it and its sequel, you can head on to the new *Atelier Ryza 3*.

169

OCTOPATH TRAVELER II

EIGHT STORIES COLLIDE FOR ANOTHER EPIC ADVENTURE

O ctopath *Traveler* was a surprise early hit on the Switch, spawning ports for other systems and a decent mobile spin-off, too. And now it has a sequel, with eight new stars and their own unique stories that thread together into one fantastic tale. The superb 2D-HD visuals are back, mixing pixel-art characters and stunning 3D scenery, while the game play just keeps getting better, with new combat mechanics and new ways to travel and interact with the people you meet. Whether or not you played the original, this is one RPG that you won't want to miss!

QUICK TIPS

BREAK AND BOOST

■ Build up your boost points from turn to turn, then use them to boost your attacks or abilities. Maximizing the damage of a heavy attack or the effect of a healing potion can make a big difference.

USE YOUR LATENT POWERS

■ Every hero has his or her own Latent Power, which you can unleash when you've filled your gauge. Use them in tricky fights where the odds are stacked against you—or in boss battles.

DAY AND NIGHT

■ You have different Path Actions in the sequel, depending on whether it's day or night. If you're struggling to move forward in the daytime, why not see what you can do after sunset?

HIT THE ROAD!

■ *Octopath Traveler II* doesn't focus on one hero or one story. Instead, it stars an oddball ensemble of warriors, merchants, scholars, thieves, and priests, each with their own skills and goals. Of course, their tales intertwine, and you'll find plenty of moments when your favorites journey and battle together.

Osvald
Fascinating.

THE WARRIOR
■ The younger prince of Ku, Hikari is a skillful swordsman looking for allies to help him end his country's wars. By day he can challenge those he meets to duels and learn their skills. By night, he hands out bribes for information.

THE DANCER
■ Agnea dreams of stardom, leaving her country home in search of her big break. In the daytime, she can use her allure to attract the townsfolk and bind them to help her in battle. When night falls, her Entreat power will encourage them to gift her useful items.

THE SCHOLAR
■ Osvald began life as a scholar, but framed for the murder of his wife and daughter, he's spent the past five years in a prison cell. Now he's out and looking for revenge. A master detective, he can scrutinize the townspeople for information, but at night Osvald's dark side can emerge.

Throné
I'll take that.

THE THIEF
■ Throné is a member of the Blacksnakes thieves guild, roaming the city in search of stuff to steal. When the cops or rival gangs get too close, she can surprise them with an ambush, but during daylight hours she keeps busy picking pockets.

FAST FACT

Octopath Traveler: Champions of the Continent isn't just another mobile spin-off, but a full-on prequel to *Octopath Traveler*. It even features key characters from the first game.

LIKE THIS? TRY THIS:

CHAINED ECHOES
■ Like *Octopath Traveler* and the *Bravely Default* games, *Chained Echoes* is a throwback to classic 1990s JRPGs with some modern twists thrown in. It's got cool heroes, a great story, and a vast world to explore.

ONE PIECE ODYSSEY

Things are rough for Monkey D. Luffy and his Straw Hat Pirate crew. Marooned on a mysterious island full of hostile creatures, they have lost their pirate skills and powers—and they've also lost their ship! Can they recover their missing abilities and repair the *Thousand Sunny*, or will they be trapped forever on their new island home?

It's a story that'll take you to some unexpected places—not to mention some familiar scenes from the original manga books and anime cartoons. If you love *One Piece* and classic turn-based RPGs, you'll find this *Odyssey* a treat!

QUICK TIPS

MAKE CAMP
■ Use every chance you get to make a camp. You can recharge the crew, stock up on meals and trick balls, change outfits, and check your encyclopedia.

USE MONKEY'S REACH
■ Monkey's rubbery arms are your greatest asset. Look out for points that he can grapple to, and items in high places that only Monkey's hands can grab!

TRY AUTO BATTLE AND SPEED UP
■ There's so much fighting in *One Piece Odyssey* that it can become a grind. Try turning on Auto Battle and Speed Up in the Tactics menu to keep things moving.

SHIPWRECKED!

■ With their ship, the *Thousand Sunny*, almost destroyed by a violent storm, the Straw Hat crew seek refuge on the island of Waford. You'll need to explore the island and its ancient ruins if you want to get your crew shipshape and back on the rolling sea.

TUNNELS AND TOWERS
■ Waford was once home to an ancient civilization. Who knows what you might find in its dusty and dangerous ruins, its underground caverns, and the central towers that soar up into the sky?

Find Lim

FIGHT TO SURVIVE
■ From its giant apes to its monster snails, the local wildlife is looking to exterminate your crew. You better recover your battling skills, or you won't make it off alive!

FRIENDS OR FOES?
■ The island is deserted except for a young woman, Lim, and a bold explorer, Adio. Both have powers that can aid the Straw Hat Pirates—but will they be your allies or your enemies?

MIGHTY GUARDIANS
■ Powered by ancient magic, stone colossi haunt the ruins and the jungles. What secrets do they guard, and can your crew defeat them in battle?

FAST FACT

The *One Piece* manga has featured in Japan's *Weekly Shonen Jump* magazine for over twenty-six years, and now occupies over one hundred volumes of collected *One Piece* books.

UNIQUE SKILLS

■ Luffy isn't the only Straw Hat Pirate with useful skills. Zoro's blade can chop through barriers, while Sanji is an awesome cook who can track down ingredients even when they're buried underground. Chopper has healing abilities, and can fit into tunnels and reach areas that the bigger pirates can't fit into. Try switching to Chopper if you're stuck!

STRAW HAT SKIRMISH

■ While it's an easy-going game, *One Piece Odyssey* has a surprisingly complex battle system. If you're finding it hard to get your head around it, these tips might help.

TAKE YOUR TURN
■ Each pirate, ally, or enemy takes a turn in battle. When it's a pirate's turn, you can command them to attack an enemy, use an item, or use one of their skills.

KNOW YOUR TYPES
■ Each pirate or enemy has an attack type, which works a bit like rock, paper, scissors. Power types do extra damage against Speed types, who are strong against Technique types. But Technique types are tougher against Power types. Use this when setting targets for your pirates.

Dragon Twister!

SKILLS
■ Skills can be special attacks that dish out huge amounts of damage to one or more enemies, or perks that heal, protect, or buff another member of the crew. Skills use Tension Points, and may have extra effects, adding extra bleeding or burning damage, or temporarily paralyzing the target.

SKILL-UP AND ACCESSORIZE

■ Leveling up happens automatically, but by collecting skill fragments you can power up your pirate skills. Remember to do so every time you find them—it could help you win your next fight!

■ Badges and other accessories boost your offensive and defensive stats. Use them to fix a character with weak stats or make your biggest damage dealers even more powerful!

Tempo!

OWN THE ZONE
■ Most battles also take place between two zones, with one group fighting in one zone and the other fighting in the second. It makes sense to keep pirates fighting against enemies of a weaker type, and you can move them to attack in a different zone.

THANKS FOR THE MEMORIES!

■ As the game goes on, you'll find that this odyssey isn't just about exploring Waford—it's about exploring the Straw Hat Pirates' past! This gives you the chance to relive some of the biggest moments of the *One Piece* saga, though they might play out differently this time!

BACK IN ALABASTA

■ Remember the Alabasta kingdom and Monkey B. Luffy's battles against the Baroque Works? This is your chance to explore the city and the deserts beyond, and take on the fiendish Crocodile.

Chopper

Oh! Is this Alabasta?

OLD FRIENDS

■ It's also a chance to catch up with friends and pirate family. Want to hang out with Princess Vivi, or see Luffy's heroic brother one more time?

BOUNTIES AND BATTLES

■ Luffy's memories aren't short of action. There are side quests to complete and bounties to claim by slaying criminals and monsters. Your old enemies aren't keen to see you, either!

LIKE THIS? TRY THIS:

DRAGON BALL Z: KAKAROT

■ The greatest *Dragon Ball Z* game does its best to cover the series' biggest story lines, with visuals straight from the anime and plenty of epic one-on-one duels!

Hero of **Hyrule**

Is *Tears of the Kingdom* the final chapter in the *Legend of Zelda* saga?

■ By the time of *Tears of the Kingdom*, Link has been the legendary hero of Hyrule for thousands and thousands of years. But how did Link's story start, and is *Tears of the Kingdom* its final chapter? Here's what you need to know.

The legend begins

■ Long before there was a Link or Zelda, the goddess Hylia protected the land of Hyrule and its greatest secret: a magic of incredible power known as the Triforce. Sadly, evil forces searching for the Triforce destroyed the realm, leaving only shattered fragments, still protected by the goddess and floating in the sky.

■ Many years later, a young woman from the community of Skyloft is kidnapped by a self-styled demon lord, who believes she's the key to resurrecting his fiendish master. Her best friend, a knight of Skyloft, descends to the broken lands below to save her. He succeeds, but sets a new chain of events in motion. Evil will return to Hyrule, and Link and Zelda will return to fight it. This is the tale of the *Legend of Zelda: Skyward Sword*.

FAST FACT

Not every Zelda game fits inside the main timeline of the saga. Many of the mobile games, like *Link's Awakening* and *A Link Between Worlds*, are now officially part of an alternative "Fallen Hero" timeline, with different villains to battle and worlds to explore.

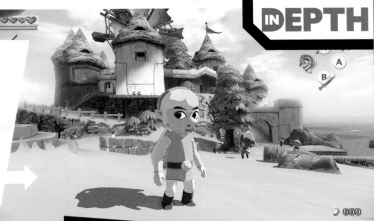

The legend continues

■ This cycle repeats over many different tales and lifetimes. Link might change from a bold young knight in green to a younger boy, and Hyrule itself will change from a rich fantasy kingdom to a cursed land where monsters roam. It's even submerged beneath the sea! Yet every time evil tries to destroy Hyrule and take the Triforce, new versions of Link and Zelda emerge to stop it in its tracks.

Calamity strikes

■ *Breath of the Wild* comes right toward the end of the saga (so far). By this point, Hyrule has developed into an advanced civilization, powered by the magical technology of the ancient Sheikah culture. Threatened by a new evil, Calamity Ganon, the people of Hyrule created four Divine Beasts to weaken him, so that he could be sealed away. But, thousands of years later, Calamity Ganon returns. He defeats Hyrule's guardians, including its greatest hero, Link, and is only stopped when

Princess Zelda seals both her spirit and his in Hyrule Castle. You can see this play out in *Hyrule Warriors: Age of Calamity*.

■ A century passes, and Link awakens to find Hyrule in ruin, with only scattered villages and settlements remaining, and monsters stomping across the land. But by working with the people of Hyrule and the spirits of its former champions, he's able to reboot the Divine Beasts, battle a resurrected Ganon, and help Zelda lock him away once more.

Tears of the Kingdom

■ You might think the legend ends there, but beneath Hyrule lies yet another force of darkness, rising again to shatter the kingdom and send a monstrous army to murder its protectors. Is this the game that brings Link's legend full circle, or does it take it to its final conclusion? You'll have to play the *Legend of Zelda: Tears of the Kingdom* to find out!

ASTERIGOS: CURSE OF THE STARS

ADVENTURES IN A CITY OF MAGIC, MYTH, AND LEGEND

QUICK TIPS

It might have come from a small indie studio, but *Asterigos* is a game with big ambitions! This action-adventure mixes the mighty bosses and challenging combat of a *Dark Souls* game with the exploration and cartoon style of a *Legend of Zelda*, and it's every bit as exciting as that sounds.

As Hilda, brave warrior of the Northwind Legion, you follow your heroic father to the mysterious city of Aphes. Dark forces hold the city and your poor pops hostage, and only you can defeat them, using your weapons and the powers of the gods. Monsters walk the streets and stalk the plazas, so get ready for a fight!

ROLL WITH THE PUNCHES

■ Enemy attacks hit hard, so use your roll move to dodge them and your shield blocks and weapon parries to stop them hitting home.

EMPTY THE CHESTS

■ Some alleys and pathways seem to lead nowhere, but look carefully. Could that dim alcove or breakable barricade hide a chest full of loot?

MIX YOUR WEAPONS

■ You can have two weapons active at a time, so try switching them around. Daggers are fast, but you can keep foes at a distance with a spear!

HERO OF APHES

■ Evil magic, wicked cults, and a hunger for cursed stardust have transformed many of the citizens of Aphes into monsters. Those that remain hide out in underground crypts and shelters, hoping for a hero who can save the day. Hilda is that hero, with the fighting skills to battle Aphes's biggest bullies and bosses, though she can always learn new abilities and elemental powers.

SAVE THE CITY

■ Once you've made your way into Aphes, you'll be working with Minerva, Aphes's former ruler. Your missions will take you to every area of the city and some beyond, searching for important citizens and sacred items that could turn the battle in your favor.

MASTER ELEMENTAL MAGIC

■ You start the game with six powerful weapons, but to defeat the powers of evil, you'll need to master elemental magic. Each enemy is vulnerable to either fire, ice, astral, or thunder energy, and you can combine these powers with your attacks to beat them faster!

FIGHT EVIL

■ Fight the monsters and the bosses and you'll gain experience and gather stardust. Stardust can be used to upgrade your weapons, while experience levels you up, allowing you to upgrade your health and attacks—and get points to learn new abilities.

THE STORY CONTINUES

■ The game doesn't end when you finish the story. There's not only a more challenging New Game Plus mode, but a new chapter, *Call of the Paragons*, which pits Hilda against the restless spirits of the old heroes of Aphes!

FAST FACT

Asterigos has ten secret bosses that only appear after the Trinity Night event. You'll need to search high and low through the city to find them, or speak to shady characters lurking around the streets.

LIKE THIS? TRY THIS:

IMMORTALS: FENYX RISING

■ Looking for more action and adventure with a mythological theme? *Immortals: Fenyx Rising* is a seriously underrated gem, with vast lands to explore in a battle to save the Greek gods!

BLUE PROTOCOL

IT'S TIME TO GET YOUR PARTY STARTED!

What if you took the awesome storytelling and anime style of Bandai Namco's beloved *Tales* series and made a multiplayer online RPG with hints of *Destiny* and *Genshin Impact*? Well, that's what Bandai Namco and Amazon have done with the brilliant *Blue Protocol*.

The game takes players on a journey through the world of Regnas, where magic and technology have worked together for thousands of years to create a landscape full of wonder. Sadly, using too much tech has taken its toll on this world, and war and disaster threaten to tear it apart. Only a brave band of heroes can prevent a catastrophe and put Regnas to rights. Will you join them? Since the game is free to play, you'd be daft not to!

QUICK TIPS

CHAIN YOUR MOVES
■ Your combat moves are designed to be chained together. Use a charge attack to knock enemies off-balance, then hit them hard with follow-up moves.

STAY CLASSY
■ The different classes have different roles. If you're playing multiplayer, use abilities that benefit your team and see if there are ways in which your skills can work together. Can your Keen Strider support your team's Twin Striker with heals and buffs?

CHECK THE LIST
■ *Blue Protocol*'s dungeons can be tackled solo, but they can be tough for just one hero. It's sometimes easier to open up the party list and find a party tackling the same dungeon. You might even make some friends for future fights!

RAGE IN REGNAS

■ You can play through *Blue Protocol* solo, but it's twice as much fun when you join forces with your friends!

CLOSE-COMBAT CLASSES

■ *Blue Protocol* has five classes. The Blade Warden uses sword and shield to defend the party, while the Twin Striker's fierce, spinning axe attacks can cut a path through gangs of monsters. Trust the Foe Breaker to smash them with their earth-shaking hammer, which doubles as a cannon!

RANGED-COMBAT CLASSES

■ The Keen Strider supports the party from a distance with their bow-and-arrow skills and healing capabilities. The Spell Weaver is too weak for frontline action, but brutally effective at a distance with their magical fire blasts and blizzards.

DEADLY RAIDS AND DUNGEONS

■ Regnas's most dangerous areas are its dungeons, where the game's key quests come alive. You can take them on solo, bring a party of three friends, or use matchmaking and the parties list to find a party to play with. The bigger raids pitch multiple parties against the game's mightiest monsters!

ECHOES

■ You can find Echoes while exploring Regnas, or craft them yourself. Use them to summon hugely powerful creatures when you need to soften up a tough enemy—or finish them before they finish you!

FAST FACT

Think *Blue Protocol* looks like a *Tales* game? Members of the team worked on the epic RPG series, and you can see key elements from favorite *Tales* heroes in the character customization options.

LIKE THIS? **TRY THIS:**

DESTINY 2

■ While there's a lot of *Genshin Impact* in *Blue Protocol*, the mix of classes and solo and co-op play reminds us of *Destiny 2*. Prefer sci-fi and guns to sword and sorcery? This is going to be your jam.

TRANSFORMERS: REACTIVATE

Forget robots in disguise—this is all-out war!

Earth has fallen. The world has been overrun by an army of malevolent Cybertronians known as The Legion, and the last remnants of mankind face certain doom. Yet a team of plucky warriors and scientists have other ideas. They're finding and reactivating Autobots—the great robot defenders of Humanity—in the hope of building a Transformer resistance. In *Transformers: Reactivate*, you're that resistance, playing with up to three friends in glorious co-op to fight The Legion and save the world.

■ The Legion came without warning to decimate Earth's cities, destroying all resistance. Only small groups of human fighters carry on the battle for survival.

■ The Legion's robots come in many forms, and they don't only dominate the streets. These bad boys have seized control of the skies, making things tricky for your reawakened Transformers crew.

FAST FACT

We've had *Transformers* video games for almost as long as we've had *Transformers*. The first, *Transformers: The Battle to Save the Earth*, came out in 1986 on the Commodore 64, only two years after the first *Transformers* "G1" TV series.

■ This hulking Legion monster isn't any kind of familiar Transformer. It smashes through armored vehicles like they're toys!

■ *Reactivate* is a return to the gritty, all-action game play of the *Transformers: War for Cybertron* and *Fall of Cybertron* games, after the cartoon brawling of *Transformers: Devastation* and the squad-based strategy of *Transformers: Battlegrounds.*

■ Mankind's last hope? To reactivate the surviving Autobots, up to four of you can join the fight against The Legion, playing as fan favorites like Bumblebee, Ratchet, and Ironhide. Don't be surprised if The Legion has some Decepticon enemies as well!

183

One ring to rule them all

One can simply walk into Mordor with these awesome Middle-earth games!

J. R. R. Tolkien's world of Middle-earth has been inspiring game developers since the earliest days of video games. The 1980s home computers like the Commodore 64 and Sinclair ZX Spectrum had incredible text adventures based on *The Hobbit* and *Lord of the Rings*, while the arrival of the Peter Jackson movie trilogy in 2001 kicked off a new wave of action and strategy games.

Since then we've had massive multiplayer RPGs in the style of *World of Warcraft*, epic fantasy adventures, and games where you could take on the might of Mordor with an army of your own. We've even seen Middle-earth in Lego form, thanks to adaptations of the *Lord of the Rings* trilogy and Peter Jackson's later *Hobbit* films.

And the Middle-earth action isn't stopping, with the new *Lord of the Rings: Gollum* and *Lord of the Rings: Return to Moria* games. If you fancy an adventure in Tolkien's legendary world, you've got a great bunch of games to get into!

Middle-earth Classics

The best of forty years of Tolkien games

THE HOBBIT

1982

■ This ancient text adventure had simple game play and barely any graphics, but it managed to convince the gamers of the 1980s that they were exploring a living, breathing Middle-earth. It had some really challenging puzzles, plus a bunch of dwarves who kept singing about gold.

LORD OF THE RINGS: THE TWO TOWERS

2002

■ Electronic Arts used the second *Lord of the Rings* movie as the basis for an all-action game starring Aragorn, Legolas, and Gimli. It did a brilliant job of re-creating all the epic moments of the film and was followed up by *Return of the King*, which did the same for the third movie.

LORD OF THE RINGS: BATTLE FOR MIDDLE-EARTH

2004

■ Having given the movies the action game treatment, Electronic Arts used them again as inspiration for a series of strategy games. The first let you play through the biggest battles of the movies, with Aragorn, Gandalf, Saruman, and the ring wraiths all leading their troops into war.

FAST FACT

The Two Towers and *Return of the King* were so successful that Electronic Arts followed them up with another game. *War in the North* followed three all new heroes as they battled Sauron's forces in the North of Middle-earth.

LORD OF THE RINGS ONLINE

2007

■ This was one of a wave of massive multiplayer online games that appeared after *World of Warcraft*—and one of the best! You could create your own hero and wander through some of the most famous (and notorious) places in Middle-earth. Amazingly, it's still going strong today.

LORD OF THE RINGS: ARAGORN'S QUEST

2010

■ *Aragorn's Quest* restaged the three *Rings* movies as an action-adventure with Aragorn in the starring role. When you weren't battling Nazgul on Weathertop or Sauron's armies in Minas Tirith, weird side quests had you playing as Sam's son, Frodo, preparing a part for the king.

LEGO THE LORD OF THE RINGS

2012

■ After *Star Wars*, *Harry Potter*, *Batman*, and *Indiana Jones*, it was only natural that the Traveller's Tales *Lego* series would take on *Lord of the Rings*. It's another brick blockbuster with great action and hilarious takes on the big movie scenes. *Lego The Hobbit* followed in 2014.

MIDDLE-EARTH: SHADOW OF MORDOR

2014

■ This darker take on Middle-earth introduced a new hero, Talion the ranger, as he fights against the forces of Sauron in the period just before *Lord of the Rings*. Too grim and violent for younger gamers, it was followed by an even more epic sequel, *Shadow of War* in 2017.

Lord of the Rings: Gollum

■ We've had games starring Frodo, Aragorn, Legolas, and Gandalf, but this might be the first Middle-earth game to focus entirely on Gollum. *Lord of the Rings: Gollum* follows the villainous creature from his time lurking in the depths beneath Sauron's fortress to his adventures in Mirkwood, the Misty Mountains, and beyond.

■ The game features its own version of the character, rather than the one played by Andy Serkis in the movies, and there's plenty of stealth, sneaking, and puzzle solving to be done as Gollum works his way through orcs, elves, trolls, and ring wraiths—not to mention some familiar faces from *Lord of the Rings*.

Lord of the Rings: Return to Moria

How do you fancy joining Gimli as he attempts to retake Moria after the events of *Lord of the Rings*? That's exactly what's going on in this new game of exploration, crafting, and survival. You can work together with up to eight of your mates, delving deep into the ruins of Khazad-dûm (as the dwarves call it) in search of its ancient treasures.

SURVIVE THE MINES
■ Of course, there will be dangers. The ruins and the mines themselves are treacherous, with crumbling stairs and walkways, flooded caverns, and terrifying drops.

RETAKE THE CITY
■ Orcs, trolls, and goblins also lurk in the depths of the old dwarven city. Different factions are fighting with each other—but they're still happy to slay any wandering dwarves. You had better be on your guard!

MINE AND CRAFT
■ If you know dwarves, you know they love metalwork. Mine for silver, iron, gold, and mithril, and you'll soon be crafting the weapons, armor, and dwarven gadgets you'll need to survive and thrive. By discovering ancient dwarven crafting recipes, you'll be able to fight off every peril, and even start rebuilding Khazad-dûm.

MORE TO EXPLORE
■ The world is generated for each adventure using clever procedural algorithms, just like *Minecraft*, so no two runs through Moria are going to be the same!

Exoprimal

It's Iron Man versus the dinosaurs. What's not to love?

■ Okay, so *Exoprimal* isn't really Tony Stark taking on the T. Rex, but it's as close as you're going to get. Interdimensional vortexes are literally raining dinosaurs onto Earth. Luckily, an advanced AI, Leviathan, has the solution: sending a team of men and women in high-tech exosuits to wipe out the massive man-eating dinos. But can you trust Leviathan, or is the AI up to no good? That's what you and your Hammerhead crew are going to find out!

Meet the Hammerheads

■ *Exoprimal* is designed around five-player online co-op play, with each player taking on a different member of the mighty Hammerheads. You'll be sent out to battle the dinos across eight types of missions, ranging from hunting down specific dinosaurs to beating enemy teams in battle.

FAST FACT

Capcom has history with dinosaurs, having cranked out three *Dino Crisis* games between 1999 and 2003. These much-loved games were pretty scary, mixing the survival horror of *Resident Evil* with the dinos of *Jurassic Park*.

Guard the group

■ Each of your exosuits comes with different weapons and gadgets. The Roadblock suit has the heaviest armor and comes with a shield to protect both you and your teammates from those supersize jaws and claws.

Even deadlier dinos

■ You're not facing just normal dinosaurs. Passing through a vortex can mutate these monster lizards, transforming them with new powers that they can use to turn you from a robot-suited warrior into a crunchy snack.

Going toe-to-claw

■ Assault Suits like Murasame and Zephyr are designed for players that want to get in close to slice and dice their way through the dinosaur horde. Sure, you're making them extinct all over again, but they're trying to do the same to you!

Taking on neo T. Rex

■ One mission puts you up against your ultimate opponent: a mutated "neo" T. Rex. Throw everything you've got against this bad boy. He can take a lot of punishment, and his roar isn't worse than his bite!

HOGWARTS LEGACY

MAGICAL TIMES AT A MAGICAL SCHOOL

ogwarts Legacy lets you live the dream of enrolling as a Hogwarts student. Only you're no ordinary student. For one thing, you're a late starter, joining the school in the fifth year with just basic instruction from your mentor, Professor Fig. For another, you can see an ancient magic that other wizards or witches can't—and that's making you a target for a cabal of dark wizards, witches, and renegade goblins. Where your fellow students just have to pass their O.W.L.s, you have to fight to survive!

Luckily, you have some good teachers looking after you, and some new best friends to help you on your way. Brush up on your skills with spells and potions, and you'll uncover the mysteries of Hogwarts and make it through the year.

QUICK TIPS

FOLLOW THE TRAIL
■ Hogwarts's maze of corridors and stairways gets confusing, so make sure you have your next quest active, then use your magic compass and follow the trail of golden sparks to find the way.

OPEN THE EYE CHESTS
■ There's some good stuff hidden in the Eye Chests dotted around Hogwarts, but you can't open them if the eyes can see you. Try using the Disillusionment charm to get close without getting seen.

SELL YOUR UNWANTED GEAR
■ You've only got a limited amount of space in your inventory, so sell your unwanted gear and items to clear some room. You'll also make money you can spend on things you really need.

BACK IN TIME TO HOGWARTS

■ *Hogwarts Legacy* is set in the legendary School of Witchcraft and Wizardry, but not as you know it. At roughly one hundred years before the Harry Potter novels, it's long before Albus Dumbledore became headmaster. You might recognize the names—and some of the ghosts—but the teachers and the students are a very different bunch!

GRADE A STUDENT

■ You've come to Hogwarts to learn—and you'll need all the magical skills you can get. Attend your Potions, Charms and Herbology classes, and keep practicing Defense Against the Dark Arts.

SECRET MISSIONS

■ While you're not studying, Professor Fig and his allies need your help with a deeper mystery at the heart of Hogwarts. What links long-dead wizards and witches with a book hidden beneath the library and a secret vault at Gringotts Bank?

FAST FACT

At the time of *Hogwarts Legacy*, the headmaster is Phineas Nigellus Black. He's the great-great-grandfather of Sirius Black III from *Harry Potter and the Prisoner of Azkaban*.

ADD HORKLUMP JUICE

SNEAKING OUT

■ Sometimes doing the right thing means breaking a few rules. Your friends can help you sneak around the corridors and even get you inside forbidden areas of the school or its library. Just watch out for Peeves and the other ghosts—they love to get you into trouble!

POTION MASTER

■ Spells and charms will get you so far, but you'll need potions to heal, boost your defense and damage, turn invisible, or call up a fearsome storm. You can learn how in your Potions classes, then get the ingredients and start brewing up your own!

Peeves: Sebastian Sallow and his new little friend, out exploring where they shouldn't be!

HEADING OUT OF HOGWARTS

■ There's more to *Hogwarts Legacy* than lessons and the school. If you want to find out what's really going on, then you'll have to explore the area outside Hogwarts's walls and get to know the locals!

HIT THE STORES

■ Head to Hogsmeade to fill up on potion ingredients, conjuration recipes, herbology seeds, and the latest wizard or witch wear. Or why not stop for a pint of Butterbeer or get a haircut? Just watch out for any bad guys lurking.

FANTASTIC BEASTS

■ You'll encounter weird and wonderful creatures as you venture beyond Hogwarts. Some need help or protection from poachers, while others want to make you their next snack. Look after the magical critters and they might find ways to help you in return.

HAMLETS AND HIGHLANDS

■ The different regions around Hogwarts are also yours to explore, covering large stretches of the Scottish Highlands, tiny hamlets, the Forbidden Forest, coastal caves, and more. Who knows what treasure vaults, wizard trials, and deadly dungeons you're going to find?

TAKE A RIDE

■ Getting around these larger spaces could take hours on foot! Luckily, it's not long before you have a broomstick to ride around on, or you could even make friends with a Hippogriff or Graphorn and ride them. Now that's traveling in style!

MAKING FRIENDS

■ Both in and out of classes, you'll make friends with young witches and wizards from all of Hogwarts's houses. They'll help you explore the area around Hogwarts and track down new locations, and they'll also battle by your side in duels. Think carefully about how you treat them—kindness and loyalty will often be repaid.

DUELS AND BATTLES

◾ Magical guardians, rebel goblins, grumpy trolls, and dark wizards—they're all out to get you, even though you're a kid! You'll have to master the skills of dueling and defense to live another day!

CAST AWAY!
◾ Your basic "cast" spell does a small amount of damage but can't get through Protego shields or do much to hurt the larger monsters.

PROTECT YOURSELF
◾ Practice timing your Protego spells, so that they shield you from enemy attacks. Watch out for heavy attacks or getting surrounded, though. Sometimes it's better to dodge and hit right back with a spell of your own!

BREAK THEIR GUARD
◾ Spells like Levioso, Depulso, and Accio are great for surprising an enemy or breaking their defenses ready for a follow-up attack. Hurling objects at them with your magic also works!

ATTACK!
◾ Stringing spells together in chains of casts and the more powerful Glacius, Descendo, or Incendio spells can end a battle quickly. Keep juggling enemies in the air to keep them off the offensive. Later on in the game, you'll unlock some more vicious spells, including some infamous unforgivable curses. Is it right to use Crucio or Avada Kedavra against a foe who wants you dead?

LIKE THIS? TRY THIS:

LEGO HARRY POTTER COLLECTION
◾ If you want to relive the magic of the Harry Potter movies, this brilliant Lego Harry Potter bundle covers everything from year one through to the Deathly Hallows in awesome brick-busting style.

TOP 10

CREEPY GAMES

Looking for a creepy tale with blood-curdling scares and terrifying monsters? These games are guaranteed to give you the shivers!

GELATI

★★★
★★★
???

0/1

10 Penko Park

■ OK, so it's not all that scary, but Ghostbutter's phantom photography game definitely qualifies as spooky. Alone in an abandoned wildlife park, it's up to you to explore and capture its ghostly critters in your snapshots. Some can be hard to spot, while others aren't quite as cuddly as they seem! *Penko Park* owes a lot to *Pokémon Snap*, but its cute and creepy style, spooky tunes, and imaginative creatures make it more than just a clone.

AVAILABLE ON: Nintendo Switch, PC

09 Poppy Playtime

■ Once upon a time, Playtime Co. was the best toy factory of them all. Now it's all but abandoned—apart from the killer toys looking for revenge! From creepy dolls to the horrifying Huggy Wuggy, they're looking to catch you and play in their own deadly way. Only your puzzle-solving abilities and your high-tech GrabPack can hold them off. With some genuinely terrifying moments, this is one seriously scary game.

AVAILABLE ON: PC, iOS, Android

08 Among the Sleep (Enhanced Edition)

■ How frightening can a game where you play a toddler with a talking teddy be? Plenty, it turns out, when that game is *Among the Sleep*. Waking up in the night, two-year-old David wants his mommy, but she's nowhere to be found. Only by exploring a weirdly familiar nightmare world can he and Teddy find his missing memories and get to safety. There aren't many games that can put you in the tiny shoes of a young kid with all their fears, but *Among the Sleep* does it brilliantly.

AVAILABLE ON:
Nintendo Switch, PS4, Xbox One, PC

07 Yomawari: Night Alone

■ Picture the scene: a young girl is out walking her dog at twilight, when something awful happens and the dog disappears. Worse, her older sister goes out to look for the lost pooch, only to go missing, too! There's nothing left but to venture out into a town turned strange, where ghosts and demons stalk the streets, doing their best to hunt you down. This creepy Japanese adventure is incredibly atmospheric and spooky, and started off a series that keeps dishing up the scares!

AVAILABLE ON: **Nintendo Switch, PC**

06 Limbo

■ This weird 2D platform game is one of the most influential indie games of all time, and although it's now over ten years old, it doesn't seem to have aged one day! If the black-and-white cartoon style doesn't freak you out, the giant spiders and terrifying traps definitely will—and the gruesome deaths your hero endures when you get it wrong mean this isn't a game for younger kids. However, if you can handle the fear factor, this is one creepy classic you won't forget.

AVAILABLE ON: **Nintendo Switch, PS4, Xbox One, PC, iOS, Android**

05 Hello Neighbor II

■ The sequel to the hide-and-seek horror classic is even better, taking you back into the house of your creepy neighbor, but also letting you loose in the town of Raven Brooks. You've not just got the scary Mr. Peterson to dodge this time around, but a host of oddball characters with their own secrets to conceal, along with a mysterious figure in a crow costume who's often on your trail. Can you outfox them all and find out what's really going on? Expect some nerve-wracking moments as you find out!

AVAILABLE ON: Nintendo Switch, PS5, PS4, Xbox Series S/X, Xbox One, PC

04 Five Nights at Freddy's: Security Breach

■ The *Five Nights at Freddy's* series has been thrilling gamers for nearly ten years, pitting harassed nighttime workers against murderous animatronic creatures, using only the remote-controlled lights, doors, vents, and security cameras to keep Freddy Fazbear and his fiendish friends at bay. *Security Breach* is the ninth game in the series, but also the most ambitious, giving you a whole 1980s mall to explore as you try to survive one terrifying night.

AVAILABLE ON: PS5, PS4, Xbox Series S/X, Xbox One, PC

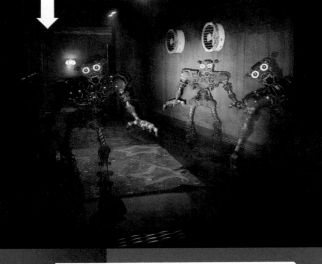

03 Little Nightmares II

■ *Little Nightmares* was one of the scariest platform and puzzle games ever, but it's a picnic in the park compared to *Little Nightmares II*! Mono, a young boy in a paper-sack mask, must work with Six, the star of the original game, to stop a transmission that's turning their whole world evil. Along the way they'll have to cross some sinister landscapes and escape from some of the most frightening enemies in games. Don't blame us if it gives you your own little nightmares!

AVAILABLE ON: Nintendo Switch, PS4, Xbox One, PC

02 Bendy and the Dark Revival

■ The sequel to the brilliant *Bendy and the Ink Machine*, *Bendy and the Dark Revival* gives you a tour of the creepiest cartoon studio ever, where the once-lovable characters have been tainted by a mysterious ink, and you'll need to use all your skills in stealth and strategy to survive them. With its haunted, old-time world and some really ghastly shocks, *Bendy and the Dark Revival* is one exceptionally scary game!

AVAILABLE ON:
PS4, Xbox One, PC

FAST FACT

theMeatly, creator of the *Bendy* games, is a comic-book artist and puppeteer, as well as a game developer. He originally had the idea for a game in a world that looked like a creepy cartoon sketch, but thought he needed a monster to inhabit it. That's how Bendy was born!

01 Luigi's Mansion 3

■ *Luigi's Mansion* isn't as heavy on the scares as other games on this list, but try telling that to Luigi, who spends the whole game looking terrified! Trapped in a haunted hotel and out to save Mario and his friends from a spooky revenge, it's up to Luigi to turn ghostbuster once again, sucking up the specters inside his Poltergust G-00. Packed with ingenious puzzles, sneaky spirits, and some awesome boss battles, this might be Luigi's finest hour.

AVAILABLE ON:
Nintendo Switch

WILD HEARTS

JOIN THE ULTIMATE MONSTER HUNT!

Wild Hearts owes a lot to *Monster Hunter*, but it's so much more than just a clone. Sure, you're a hunter fighting monsters in a fantasy version of historical Japan, but *Wild Hearts'* supersized Kemono have their own brutish charm—and you've got some cool new ways to slay them! Bring these big, bad bruisers down, and you can use their hides, bones, and guts to create new armor and weapons, and tackle even more ferocious varmints.

Wild Hearts also introduces Karakuri: a mystic art that allows hunters to construct structures and gadgets from a magical thread. Master Karakuri and you can build boxes that will send you leaping into the air, spring pads that will help you dodge monsters, and mighty walls that can block and repel a charging monster, not to mention a whole lot more. With the best weapons and armor, plus some advanced Karakuri on your side, you'll become an unstoppable monster-slaying machine!

QUICK TIPS

GET AROUND FASTER

■ Flying Vines, Wind Vortexes, and Rollers are brilliant for getting around large, mountainous areas fast. It takes effort and Karakuri threads to construct them, but they'll save you so much time!

EXPLORE EACH REGION

■ Instead of always pushing on to the next hunt, take time to explore new areas. You can find new spots where you can camp, discover and befriend Tsukumo, and grab some useful materials.

LEARN THE PATTERNS

■ Each giant Kemono has a range of attacks, but they'll usually move in a certain way and make a sound before they start each one. That's your signal to get out of the way!

PEST CONTROL

■ The country of Azuma has a serious pest problem: skyscraper-sized monsters roam the land, wrecking villages and stomping on the locals! They need someone to tackle the Kemono menace, and you're just the person for the job!

TRACK THE MONSTER

■ Spend some time by your campfire to select your next target, then head out to hunt them down. You can use your Karakuri crafting abilities to build a sort of radar tower to show you where they are!

FAST FACT

Each of the game's Kemono monsters is inspired by a real-world animal. You'll never look at a chicken the same way again after you've fought the fiendish Dreadclaw!

STRIKE FIRST, STRIKE HARD

■ When you've spotted your monster, sneak in and grab a few free strikes. Now the battle begins. Keep dodging their attacks, then rush in to hit them back while they're weak or distracted.

CHASE 'EM DOWN

■ Do enough damage and your Kemono target will head for the hills. Make sure you follow them, using your Hunter Vision to guide you on your way. Pick up more Healing Water while you're at it!

FINISH THEM OFF!

■ Keep attacking—and don't get killed—and you'll have your chance to strike a final blow. That means one less monster causing havoc, and more materials for you to craft new gear with!

KARAKURI

■ Karakuri crafting is one of the smartest ideas in *Wild Hearts*. By harvesting the mystic Karakuri Threads from trees and rocks, you can summon all sorts of useful structures and magical machines. You can even grab Threads from damaged Kemono, so don't be shy about crafting cool stuff!

BOXES AND SPRINGS

■ The most basic box Karakuri is useful for reaching higher spots than you can climb to, or launching yourself into the air to attack a monster on the ground. The spring pad is brilliant for speedy dodging.

BUILD A BULWARK

■ Put a lot of Karakuri boxes together and you can build a Bulwark—a tougher wall that can halt charging Kemono in their tracks. They're also great for hiding behind while you're trying to heal.

TIME TO FLY

■ The Flying Vines Karakuri fires a zip line you can use to cross gaps, reach a high point, or just move fast across the plains. You can even use them to surprise a monster with an aerial attack.

HIT 'EM HARD

■ More advanced Karakuri can be used to bash, smash, trap, and blast the Kemono, evening the odds against the toughest, nastiest monsters.

YOUR NEW BUDDIES

■ Finding the big Kemono hard to deal with? That's where the Tsukumo come in. These small, mechanical critters will help you if you befriend them. They'll dish out Karakuri thread and even try to protect you. Plus, they're great at distracting Kemono, so you can rush in and attack. Remember to upgrade them when you find some cogs. They'll get even better at their job!

KILLER KEMONO

■ *Wild Hearts'* headline monsters are as giant as they are terrifying. Each one makes a dangerous foe, but watch out for these mighty beasts.

KINGTUSK

■ The first seriously challenging monster in the game is a super-sized giant boar with deadly tusks. Watch out for his charges and earthquake special moves. A Bulwark could be your best defense!

LAVABACK

■ What could be so bad about a giant ape? How about a ferocious temper, pummeling fists, and a nasty habit of lobbing lava. A mean and cunning enemy.

DEATHSTALKER

■ If this mighty wolf Kemono doesn't give you the chills, nothing will. He's lightning-fast and ferocious, with the ability to summon ice with which to attack and defend itself.

DON'T FIGHT ALONE!

■ One of the best things about *Wild Hearts* is that you don't have to hunt alone. You can summon friends or fellow hunters to join you when you're starting on a hunt, or use the Hunters Gates to join another player's hunt and help them bring down a tricky beast.

LIKE THIS? TRY THIS:

MONSTER HUNTER: WORLD

■ It's more complex and harder to get into than *Wild Hearts*, but *Monster Hunter: World* is still a magnificent monster-slaying game, with an awesome collection of beasts to battle, and all the weapons you might need to do the job.

FIRE EMBLEM: ENGAGE

TAKE ON THE FIENDISH FELL DRAGON IN THE WAR OF THE EMBLEM RINGS

Wake up, lazy bones! As the Divine Dragon, protector of the kingdoms of Elyos, you've been asleep for a thousand years. And, boy, are you needed now. War is stirring between kingdoms, while undead creatures, known as the Corrupted, roam the land. Worst of all, there are rumors that your ancient enemy, Sombron the Fell Dragon, has returned, and you can't remember how to fight him! What are you going to do?

Luckily, you're not alone. Your stouthearted stewards will fight alongside you, while the four realms have their own heroes who will join you to battle the forces of evil. And by collecting the twelve Emblem Rings, you can summon the spirits of twelve legendary warriors, with their own awesome fighting skills and magical powers. With friends like these, you can handle anything!

QUICK TIPS

○ Alm B
Str +1   Dex +1

MAKE YOUR OWN RINGS
■ Bond Rings aren't as powerful as Emblem Rings, but you can forge them yourself and kit out all your favorite heroes with perks that will help them triumph in your next fight.

MEDIC!
■ Don't hit the battlefield without a bunch of healing options. Use healers, give your warriors vulneraries and potions, and equip any mages with healing staves. You can keep items handy in the convoy.

EQUIP YOUR SKILLS
■ Heroes that fight with an Emblem Ring equipped learn new skills from their Emblem buddy, but can't use them until you've selected them. Head to the Inventory menu and choose Manage Skills to make sure they're equipped.

FIGHT LIKE A DRAGON!

■ Just because you're called the Divine Dragon, you won't be flying around, grilling armies with your fiery breath. Instead, you'll be leading your friends into turn-based battles, fighting enemies attacking from the air, on horseback, or on foot. Only by combining strategy with your buddies' incredible abilities can you win each fight—and the war against Sombron!

CHARGE INTO COMBAT

■ Different heroes have different movement speeds. Some are mounted on speedy warhorses, and some of those horses can fly! What's more, mages and archers can attack from a distance so don't need to be next to their targets.

BATTLE BONDS

■ The more a hero Engages with an Emblem warrior, the closer their bond will become. With new Bond Levels, new skills become available, and your heroes will get boosts to their stats. Hit Bond Level 5, and a hero can inherit skills from their Emblem and use them without being Engaged!

ENGAGE!

■ You can equip your warriors with Emblem Rings, allowing them to Engage with the legendary Emblem heroes, and call on their powers and skills. This Engagement doesn't last forever, but it makes your heroes tougher and attacks more powerful, and even opens up some unique moves.

THE WEAPON TRIANGLE

■ *Fire Emblem: Engage* brings back the classic Fire Emblem weapon triangle, where swords beat axes, axes beat lances, and lances beat swords. It's not always obvious which type some weapons fit into, but they're color-coded, so red beats green, green beats blue, and blue beats red.

■ When you attack an enemy carrying one weapon with a weapon that beats it, there's a chance that you'll break their guard, meaning the next attack is guaranteed to hit them, too! Keep an eye on this to maximize your damage—and avoid taking too much from your foes.

CHAIN ATTACKS

■ Certain heroes have the Backup ability. Place them next to another hero and in contact with the same enemy, and they'll attack when that hero attacks. You can even team up multiple heroes and Backup heroes to chain together several attacks. It's a great way to take down enemies fast.

FAST FACT

The *Fire Emblem* games might never have been released outside of Japan if it wasn't for *Super Smash Bros*. The appearance of heroes Marth and Roy in *Super Smash Bros. Melee* left American fans wanting to know more, which made Nintendo think about translating the games for the United States!

FLYING FORTRESS

■ Between chapters of the story, you can hang out with the troops in your floating castle base, the Somniel. Make sure you head back there after every mission, as it's the perfect place to relax, train, develop bonds with your team, and upgrade your gear for the next battle.

Yunaka
Whoa, what? I got praise from the Divine One?! Zappy! I'm thrilled! Beyond thrilled!

BUILD YOUR FRIENDSHIPS

■ Chat to your heroes while they're resting between battles and you can help them with their worries, or encourage them when they've been fighting well. Picking the Support option can push their Support Rank up, meaning you both get a boost when you stand together in combat.

Anna
I bet this would be a hit with customers. Maybe as the signature dish of a restaurant...

GRAB A BITE

■ You can also boost your Support rank— and your heroes' stats—by joining them for a tasty meal. Head to the Café Terrace with the right ingredients and get your current chef to cook something tasty. You can treat up to two characters at a time, and even get some healing leftovers.

TRAIN

■ Being the Divine Dragon takes physical strength and stamina, and the best way to keep both up is exercise. Luckily, the Somniel has its own gym—the Training Grounds—where simple mini-games can boost your stats. Or why not fight in the Arena for extra experience points?

HIT THE STORES

■ Your heroes can't go into battle empty-handed, but—after the first few chapters—the Somniel will fill up its empty buildings with useful stores. Here you can buy and upgrade weapons, and even Engrave them with the magic of an Emblem. Stock up on other essentials while you're shopping.

LORD OF THE RINGS

■ The Ring Chamber is the Somniel's most important location. It's where you can inherit skills from your Emblems, forge your own Bond Rings, and merge Bond Rings to make them more powerful. You can also give your Emblem Rings a polish. It'll keep your Emblems happy and fighting fit!

GRIND FOR VICTORY

■ Finding *Fire Emblem: Engage* difficult as it goes on? Sometimes it pays to level up and return to a chapter with more power. Completing the optional Paralogue missions is a great idea. You can gain experience and improve Bond Levels, while there could be useful materials to harvest. What's more, some Paralogue missions unlock new heroes you won't find any other way.

■ The skirmish missions aren't so important, but they're another good way to level up your troops for the next battle, or try out different combos of heroes, Emblems, and skills.

EMBLEM **HEROES**

■ Recognize any of the Emblem heroes? If you know your *Fire Emblem* games, you'll find some familiar faces here.

MARTH
■ The star of the first *Fire Emblem* games is also the first Emblem you'll pair up with. He can help you dodge damage in combat, while his Divine Speed skill gives you an extra attack. Call on his Lodestar Rush special to launch seven brutal blows on the same foe!

CELICA
■ Bonded here with the Princess Céline, Celica was the young princess of Zofia in *Fire Emblem Echoes: Shadows of Valentia*. Her Holy Stance reflects damage from your hero, while her Echo skill gives them an extra attack. Her biggest power, Warp Ragnarok, allows her to teleport to an enemy and clobber them!

ROY
■ The legendary hero of *Fire Emblem: The Binding Blade* has some powerful defensive skills—they probably come from his *Super Smash Bros.* outings. He gives your hero bonus levels while Engaged, and has a useful buff to endure any hit and stay on 1 HP. His Blazing Lion attack is flat-out awesome.

MICAIAH
■ Micaiah first appeared in the Nintendo Wii classic, *Fire Emblem: Radiant Dawn*. With her stave skills and special weapons, she can turn any hero into a powerful Support hero. Her Great Sacrifice ability can restore an entire army from the brink of death!

LIKE THIS? **TRY THIS:**

THE DIOFIELD CHRONICLE
■ This strategy RPG from the markets of *Final Fantasy* isn't quite on *Fire Emblem*'s level, but it has a brilliant battle system where the action plays out in real time. It's faster-paced and a lot of fun!

GLOSSARY

4K
■ A screen or image with an ultra-high-definition resolution, giving the picture even more detail than a high-definition (HD) image.

Achievement
■ An award added to your online profile for completing goals or objectives in a game.

AI
■ Artificial intelligence. Intelligent behavior simulated by a computer to, for instance, control how enemies behave toward a player, or control other players on your team in a sports game.

Battle royale
■ A type of action game where sixty or more players are dropped onto a single, large map and fight until just one survives.

Beat-'em-up
■ A fighting game, where two or more fighters battle in hand-to-hand combat.

Boss
■ A bigger, tougher enemy that players have to fight at the end of a level or mission in a game.

Campaign
■ A series of levels or objectives connected by some kind of story, usually making up the single-player mode of a game.

CCG
■ Collectible card game. A style of game based on real-world card games, where players collect an army of cards and use them to battle other players.

Checkpoint
■ A point in a game where your progress is saved. If you die, you'll return to the checkpoint.

Combo
■ In a fighting game or action game, a series of button presses that triggers a hard-hitting attack or counterattack.

Co-op
■ A game or game mode where players can work together to complete objectives or win the game.

CPU
■ Central processing unit. The main processor of a computer or games console that does most of the work of running games.

Crafting
■ Using materials collected within a game to make useful items, armor, or weapons.

Cut scene
■ An animated sequence or video sequence in a game, used to build atmosphere or tell the story.

Destiny 2: Lightfall

DLC
■ Downloadable content. Additional items, characters, or levels for a game that you can buy and download as extras.

Easter egg
■ A secret feature or item that's been hidden in a game, either for fun or as a reward for observant fans.

Endgame
■ A part of a game that you can carry on playing after you've completed the main campaign or story.

FPS
■ First-person shooter. A style of game where players move around a map, shooting enemies from a first-person perspective, with a view straight from the hero's eyes.

GPU
■ Graphics processing unit. The chip inside a computer or console that turns instructions from the game software into 2D or 3D graphics that you can see on the screen.

Grind
■ To play through an area or section of a game over and over again to harvest loot or collect experience points and level up.

Tekken 8

Indie game
- Short for independent. A game created by a small team of developers—or even a single developer.

JRPG
- Japanese role-playing game. A Japanese-made, role-playing game with the kind of game play and graphics you'd expect from a *Final Fantasy*, *Persona*, or *Dragon Quest* game.

Level
- A portion or chapter of a game set in one area and with a beginning, an end, and a series of goals and challenges in-between.

Map
- An in-game map to help you find objectives, or a level where players can fight in a multiplayer game.

MOBA
- Multiplayer online battle arena. A multiplayer game where two teams of players select champions and go into battle for a series of objectives until one team wins.

Noob
- A new and inexperienced player without the skills and knowledge of an experienced player.

NPC
- Non-player character. A character in a game controlled by the computer. NPCs often provide help or guidance, sell goods, or help tell the story of the game.

Mario + Rabbids: Sparks of Hope

Open world
- A style of game where players are free to explore one or more large areas and try out different activities, rather than complete one level after another.

Patch
- An update to a game that fixes bugs or adds new features.

Platformer
- Platform game. A type of game where you run across a series of platforms or a challenging landscape, leaping over gaps and obstacles, and avoiding or defeating enemies in your path.

Port
- A version of a game made for one console or computer that's been converted to run on another.

PvE
- Player vs. environment. An online game or game mode where players work together to beat computer-controlled enemies.

PvP
- Player vs. player. An online game or game mode where players work against other players, either on their own or in teams.

Retro
- A game or visual style that looks back to older games from the 1980s or 1990s.

Roguelike
- A style of game where players fight through a series of randomly generated levels, killing monsters and collecting weapons and equipment.

RPG
- Role-playing game. A type of game where the player goes on an epic quest or adventure, fighting monsters, leveling up, and upgrading their equipment along the way.

Marvel's Midnight Suns

Season pass
- An add-on for a game that allows you to download and play through any expansions or DLC released after it launches.

Shoot-'em-up
- A style of game based on classic arcade games, where players work their way through waves of levels full of enemies, blasting away at them and avoiding their attacks.

Speed run
- A gaming challenge where players compete to finish a game or level in the shortest possible time.

Streaming
- Watching a video or playing a game through a live connection to the internet, rather than downloading it and then playing it from a console or computer.

VR
- Virtual reality. Playing games through a head-mounted screen with motion controls, so that it looks and feels more like you're actually in the game world.

XP
- Experience points. Points scored in a game for completing objectives, beating challenges, or killing monsters, and often used to upgrade the hero, their skills, or their equipment.